Joseph Smith

A LIPPER™/VIKING BOOK

PUBLISHED TITLES IN THE PENGUIN LIVES SERIES:

Larry McMurtry on Crazy Horse
Edmund White on Marcel Proust · Peter Gay on Mozart
Garry Wills on Saint Augustine · Jonathan Spence on Mao Zedong
Edna O'Brien on James Joyce · Douglas Brinkley on Rosa Parks
Elizabeth Hardwick on Herman Melville
Louis Auchincloss on Woodrow Wilson
Mary Gordon on Joan of Arc
Sherwin B. Nuland on Leonardo da Vinci
Nigel Nicolson on Virginia Woolf · Carol Shields on Jane Austen
Karen Armstrong on the Buddha · R. W. B. Lewis on Dante
Francine du Plessix Gray on Simone Weil
Patricia Bosworth on Marlon Brando
Wayne Koestenbaum on Andy Warhol
Thomas Cahill on Pope John XXIII
Marshall Frady on Martin Luther King, Jr.
Paul Johnson on Napoleon · Jane Smiley on Charles Dickens
John Keegan on Winston Churchill

FORTHCOMING:

Roy Blount, Jr., on Robert E. Lee
David Quammen on Charles Darwin
Bobbie Ann Mason on Elvis Presley
Kathryn Harrison on Saint Thérèse of Lisieux
Hilton Als on James Baldwin
Ada Louise Huxtable on Frank Lloyd Wright
Thomas Keneally on Abraham Lincoln
Simon Schama on Oliver Cromwell
Martin E. Marty on Martin Luther

GENERAL EDITOR: JAMES ATLAS

ROBERT V. REMINI

Joseph Smith

A Penguin Life

A LIPPER™/VIKING BOOK

VIKING
Published by the Penguin Group
Penguin Putnam Inc., 375 Hudson Street,
New York, New York 10014, U.S.A.
Penguin Books Ltd, 80 Strand, London WC2R 0RL, England
Penguin Books Australia Ltd, 250 Camberwell Road, Camberwell,
Victoria 3124, Australia
Penguin Books Canada Ltd, 10 Alcorn Avenue,
Toronto, Ontario, Canada M4V 3B2
Penguin Books India (P) Ltd, 11 Community Centre, Panchsheel Park,
New Delhi–110 017, India
Penguin Books (N.Z.) Ltd, Cnr Rosedale and Airborne Roads, Albany,
Auckland, New Zealand
Penguin Books (South Africa) (Pty) Ltd, 24 Sturdee Avenue,
Rosebank, Johannesburg 2196, South Africa

Penguin Books Ltd, Registered Offices:
Harmondsworth, Middlesex, England

First published in 2002 by Viking Penguin,
a member of Penguin Putnam Inc.

1   3   5   7   9   10   8   6   4   2

LIBRARY OF CONGRESS CATALOGING-IN-PUBLICATION DATA
Remini, Robert Vincent, 1921–
Joseph Smith / Robert V. Remini.
p.   cm.–(A Penguin life)
ISBN 0-670-03083-X
Includes bibliographical references.
1. Smith, Joseph, 1805–1844. 2. Mormons–United States–Biography.
I. Title. II. Penguin lives series.
BX8695.S6 R46 2002
289.3'092–dc21
[B]   2001056762

This book is printed on acid-free paper. ∞

Printed in the United States of America
Set in Berthold Garamond   Designed by Francesca Belanger

For John W. Wright
and
for his son
who died on September 11, 2001

PREFACE

SINCE ITS FOUNDING in the town of Fayette, Seneca County, New York, nearly two centuries ago, the Church of Jesus Christ of Latter-day Saints (LDS) has become a worldwide religion. More commonly known as the Mormon Church, it claims about eleven million members, and its branches are located throughout the United States, Europe, South America, South Africa, Japan, Korea, the Pacific Islands, New Zealand, and Australia. Its assets, according to some non-Mormon sources, exceed twenty billion dollars, and its annual income is estimated at more than five billion dollars. Its organization, operation, and fundamental beliefs are the same in the Pacific Islands as they are in Salt Lake City, the headquarters of the Church. And its membership and assets keep mounting each year.

The founder of this Church, the Prophet, Joseph Smith Jr., is unquestionably the most important reformer and innovator in American religious history, and he needs to be understood if we want to have a clearer idea about what this country was like in the Jacksonian era, just prior to the Civil War. Because he made such an enduring contribution to American life and culture and because he was influenced by the intellectual milieu and events of his time, I have made a special effort in this book to show the extent to which he and his work reflect the unique characteristics of this extraordinary age. Furthermore, I want to explain many of the factors that account for the ultimate success of Mormonism, despite unrelenting persecution, and what it was about this religion that elicited both savage hatred by some and undying devotion by others. And, of course, I wish to make available to the general reader the basic tenets of the Mormon religion, showing where it parallels and where it sharply diverges from other Christian faiths.

I should make it clear at the outset that I am not a Mormon. As such I faced several problems in writing this book, one of which involved Joseph's visions and revelations, which are crucial to an understanding of him, his Church, and the times in which he lived. After considerable thought I decided to present his religious experiences just as he described them in his writings and let readers decide for themselves to what extent they would give credence to them. I am not out to prove or disprove any of his claims. As a historian I have tried to be as objective as possible in narrating his life and work. Mormons will have no problem in believing everything Joseph related about his encounters with the divine. Others may be skeptical, but I hope they will, like me, find his life and legacy of particular importance in better appreciating how this nation developed during the early nineteenth century and how religion played such a commanding role in that process. To put it another way, Joseph Smith is the religious figure in United States history who has had the largest following, and that is true, I think, because so much of what he believed and taught resulted from the social, political, and intellectual dynamism of the Jacksonian age.

Moreover, since a good deal of the documentary evidence about this religion, its origins, and its history comes directly from Mormons, readers will also have to decide for themselves whether or not they are willing to believe what the believers themselves report. And it must be remembered that to a large extent many of these sources were intended to validate Joseph's claims, strengthen the faith of his followers, and attract the interest of nonbelievers.

Another problem I faced in writing this book was getting to know Joseph Smith intimately. In the past I have studied and written extensively on the Jacksonian era, and several of my books discuss the religious reforms of the antebellum period, which necessarily include the life and work of the Prophet. Still, I had never studied the man up close. The subjects of my several biographies have been political leaders; Smith was a different breed altogether. I daresay the problem of writing on any religious figure—Christian, Jew, Muslim, Buddhist, Hindu, whatever—is difficult, because believers see the person as somewhat sacred, and nonbelievers see him or her as strange or fake. So I had much research to do to learn all the details of Smith's life and what made him a unique individual. In this regard I was fortunate to know Lee Groberg, who started me off by sending me a copy of the videotape and script for his film *American Prophet: The Story of Joseph Smith,* which appeared on PBS, along with Heidi S. Swinton's excellently written and lavishly illustrated book of the same title.

Professionally, I was assisted enormously by Professor Richard Lyman Bushman of Columbia University, a Mormon, who provided me with several of his articles, answered some of the toughest questions I had about Joseph's teaching, and helped me become acquainted with a number of scholars at Brigham Young University (BYU), particularly those of the Joseph Fielding Smith Institute for the Study of the Church of Latter-day Saints. As a result I was invited to lecture at BYU, where I met and conducted a seminar with members of the history, philosophy, and religion departments. They subsequently inundated me with books, articles, and doctoral dissertations about their religion and its history, for which I am most grateful.

Among the men and women of that university to whom I owe a particular debt I want to single out first and foremost Scott H. Faulring of the Smith Institute, who not only answered many of my questions about the Mormon Church via E-mail but out of his kindness and generosity presented me with copies of Smith's seven-volume *History of the Church,* two volumes of selections from the *Encyclopedia of Mormonism,* his own edition of *An American Prophet's Record: The Diaries and Journals of Joseph Smith,* and the complete *Encyclopedia of Mormonism* on a CD-ROM. To me he is the embodiment of Mormon virtues.

Ronald K. Esplin, director of the Smith Institute, gave me several boxes of valuable documentary material, including *The Papers of Joseph Smith,* edited by Dean C. Jessee. In addition he sent along his doctoral dissertation on the emergence of Brigham Young's Mormon leadership following Smith's assassination. William C. Hartley also provided me with several copies of his articles that had been published in various Mormon journals, and Grant Underwood gave me a copy of his *The Millenarian World of Early Mormonism* and arranged for my visit to BYU. I owe a particular debt to John W. Welch, law professor at BYU and editor-in-chief of *BYU Studies,* who kindly read selected pages of my manuscript and offered suggestions to help clarify certain areas of Mormon belief. I am most grateful to all the members of the BYU faculty for their interest and assistance.

When I set out to write this book I went to the local LDS chapel in my neighborhood and asked to purchase copies of *The Book of Mormon, The Pearl of Great Price,* and *Doctrine and Covenants,* the three basic documents of the Mormon faith, but was told there were none for sale. A week or two later Lynn Johnson, a patriarch of the Church, came to my house and formally presented me with a handsomely bound volume containing all three titles. I am most obliged to him and to the local ward for their generosity.

Before beginning this narrative, I want to make it very explicit that although these men helped me enormously with some of the factual data contained in this book, they in no way influenced my interpretation of the Prophet. None of them volunteered information; they simply responded to my questions and requests. The interpretation here is completely my own. Still, I want them to know how truly grateful I am for their willingness to cooperate in my efforts to treat the Prophet fairly and without prejudice. Joseph Smith Jr. deserves a respectful hearing, and I hope neither he nor the Saints at BYU and around the globe will be disappointed or offended by what is written here.

Robert V. Remini
Wilmette, Illinois

CONTENTS

Preface   *ix*

1. The Second Great Awakening   *1*

2. First Vision   *18*

3. Moroni   *40*

4. *The Book of Mormon*   *57*

5. Organizing the Church of Christ   *75*

6. Kirtland   *95*

7. Far West   *127*

8. Nauvoo   *140*

9. Assassination   *160*

Sources   *183*

Select Bibliography   *187*

Joseph Smith

Chapter 1

The Second Great
Awakening

JOSEPH SMITH JR. was born into a wildfire of religious frenzy
that raged over large parts of the United States in the early
nineteenth century and influenced virtually every aspect of
American life and thought. Called the Second Great Awakening (the first occurred in the middle of the eighteenth century),
this explosive force swept with such scalding ferocity through
western New York that the region came to be known as the
"Burned-Over District." It marked the beginning of a new and
vigorous evangelical movement that started with a series of revival meetings at the turn of the century and reached its zenith
in the 1820s and 1830s, the years Joseph Smith Jr. was born
and raised and grew to maturity. The countryside was engulfed
by the fires of repeated revivals in which itinerant preachers
of little education but mesmerizing oratory summoned sinners to repent and reform their lives. Emotional orgies resulted, reaching such heights that they generated wild scenes
of men and women weeping and tearing their hair, vocally
confessing their sins, beating their breasts, rolling on the
ground, crawling on all fours like dogs, and barking at trees
where they had presumably cornered the devil. Some of these
preachers were given names by their detractors that were meant
to match their antics, names such as Jumpin' Jesus or Crazy Dow
or Mad Isaac. Mrs. Frances Trollope visited the United States

in 1827, stayed three and a half years, and wrote a critical book published in 1832 called *The Domestic Manners of Americans*. She witnessed one of these camp meetings, and what she saw frightened her half to death. These people behaved like lunatics, she exclaimed. One minute they seemed sane, the next raving mad. She fled the scene in panic and disbelief.

Many reasons explain this religious phenomenon. Americans at the time were undergoing sudden, jolting change—again and again. In fact, the United States changed more profoundly in the thirty years from 1790 to 1820 than during any other period in its history. As a starter, Americans had just concluded a revolution in which they shucked off monarchical rule for a wholly untried governmental system. They established a republic first under the Articles of Confederation, which failed, and then under the Constitution. Shortly thereafter they formed political parties to run the government. But this "experiment in freedom," as it was called, met only contempt and disdain from European heads of state. France wanted a bribe (the X, Y, Z Affair) before recognizing American ambassadors. It also seized American ships in French ports and engaged in naval combat with U.S. vessels, precipitating the Quasi-War with France in 1797–1798, which President John Adams managed to prevent from escalating into a full-fledged war. And England was worse. It refused to abandon its forts on U.S. soil as required under the peace treaty that ended the Revolution; it armed Indians and encouraged them to attack the frontier; it seized American ships; it impressed seamen; and it issued Orders in Council that virtually stifled U.S. international trade. Exasperated, the nation declared war against Great Britain in 1812 (this is sometimes called the Second War of Independence) only to have its coastline blockaded, Washington captured, and the White House and Capitol burned. During the war one disaster followed another. Not until General Andrew Jackson won a spectacular victory at New Orleans on January 8, 1815, was the nation rescued from the disgrace of utter and complete military defeat.

Jackson's victory, in which more than two thousand professional British soldiers were killed, wounded, or captured by a "ragtag" collection of American militiamen, regulars, men of color, Indians, pirates, and townspeople, set in motion a nationalistic surge. Americans reveled in the firm knowledge that they had finally accomplished "real" recognition of their nation's independence and that they were no longer colonists or Englishmen. They developed enormous pride in their country. "*Who would not be an American?*" trumpeted *Niles' Weekly Register* in 1815. "*Long Live the republic!*"

Once the war ended, additional changes rapidly followed: the Industrial Revolution exploded within the country, allowing Americans to establish at long last an independent national domestic economy; a market revolution began the process of converting the country from a purely agricultural to an industrial society; and then a transportation revolution inaugurated the building of roads, bridges, highways, canals, and finally railroads that assisted in expanding the country across a continent. It had taken colonists one hundred and fifty years just to settle an inland area of about one hundred miles from the coastline. In less than fifty years during the first half of the nineteenth century, Americans stretched their country three thousand miles to the Pacific Ocean.

But perhaps the most important change that took place at the start of the nineteenth century was the steady evolution of the government from a republican to a democratic form. States amended their constitutions to provide universal white manhood suffrage. As a result, in 1828 this newly enfranchised mass of ordinary citizens elected as their president General Andrew Jackson, a man without a single qualification for this high office, except his fantastic popularity resulting from his military victory at New Orleans.

Small wonder that, with all these rapid, wrenching shocks and unforeseen changes taking place within just a few decades, the American people turned to religion to find stability, guidance, and comfort. Desperate and anxiety-ridden, they looked for divine help as they struggled to reshape and anchor their lives in a modern democratic society.

In their struggle they reached out to any and all religious persuasions that promised them deliverance. And the more they could respond vocally, physically, and emotionally to the oratory of the clergy at revival meetings, the more they felt the joy and comfort of divine forgiveness that guaranteed their ultimate salvation.

What had happened was the arrival of a new romantic age that succeeded the age of reason and emphasized the importance of human emotions and feelings. Such sentiments were no longer suspect or frowned upon as they had been in the past. Now they were believed to aid individuals in their search for truth and wisdom. Intuition also served as an important tool in the search. Not surprisingly this romanticism brought about a flowering of intellectual pursuits and the appearance of a number of distinguished writers who composed arguably the finest literature this country has ever produced. Novelists and poets such as James Fenimore Cooper, Nathaniel Hawthorne, Herman Melville, Edgar Allan Poe, Henry Wadsworth Longfellow, John Greenleaf Whittier, and Walt Whitman, among others, inaugurated a golden age of American literature. And such gifted artists as John James Audubon, Thomas Sully, Asher Durant, George Innes, Thomas Cole, and George Caleb Bingham created a gallery of pictorial masterpieces.

Perhaps the most obvious expression of this romantic age was the Transcendental Movement. This New England phenomenon consisted of a group of men and women whose writings celebrated a belief not only in man's goodness but in his divinity as well. The most outstanding Transcendentalists were Ralph Waldo Emerson, Henry David Thoreau, Margaret Fuller, Orestes Brownson, George Ripley, and Bronson Alcott, who argued that each individual, male or female, could "transcend" experience and reason and through intuitive contemplation discover the glories and the mysteries of the universe and hear the voice of God.

As this romantic impulse swept across the United States it helped shape American attitudes about religion. The old Puritan belief in a stern deity poised to punish sin-prone man slowly yielded to the notion that humans were created in the image of God and therefore possessed the touch of divinity that elevated them above the rest of creation. In religious terms these notions translated into the belief that every person could achieve salvation through his or her own volition by submitting to the lordship of Christ. All it took to win salvation was an act of the will and the desire to obey the commandments and lead a holy life. The idea of an elect chosen by God no longer had the same force it enjoyed in the colonial era. One simply had to hear and respond to God's call to sanctity. And the faithful who crowded into revivalist meetings came to purge themselves of their sins and open themselves to the outpourings of love and forgiveness from a merciful Godhead.

Charles Grandison Finney was the most prominent revivalist of the day and the originator of modern evangelical

Protestantism in America. He journeyed throughout New York's Burned-Over District, summoning sinners to repent. He exhorted his listeners to "aim to be holy and not rest satisfied till they are as perfect as god."

Finney provided the model for preaching during the Second Great Awakening, and he was imitated by other clergymen of many faiths whose approach to religion blended perfectly with the emerging democratic spirit of this romantic age. For the most part these revivalist preachers were filled with the Holy Spirit and bursting with passion and wonder over the Christian message of repentance, forgiveness, and love. They were individuals who could inflame an audience with their zeal and their religious commitment. Methodists and Baptists were especially attuned to this new approach to religion, and they attracted thousands of men and women from every section of the country. They appealed to ordinary people who, like themselves, had an enormous thirst for spiritual fulfillment. Their churches swelled in number throughout the century and dominated the western and southern states.

One interesting aspect of this religious excitement was the degree to which many Americans resorted to various forms of folk magic in expressing their religious beliefs. They used such things as amulets, talismans, divining rods, and seerstones or peepstones (akin to the crystal balls used by fortune-tellers) for protection or to predict the future, or even to hunt for treasure. There was an interest in and practice of divination, personal visions, astrology, alchemy, and all manner of things occult. These people believed in devils and witches as well as angels and divine messengers. And nothing in their occult practices was regarded as contrary to accepted Christian values or beliefs. It was a generation of seekers in search of a faith by which they could govern their lives to the satisfaction of the

Almighty. And they believed fervently in Christ's imminent Second Coming, more so than any generation before or since. Armageddon was close at hand, they insisted, and salvation was of immediate concern and need. Thus, if amulets and talismans could assist them in their quest for redemption and a better life, so be it.

During the first half of the nineteenth century, countless sects and other permutations of Christian belief suddenly appeared, bringing with them an assortment of new messages that allegedly had divine sanction. These messages frequently conveyed the idea of a New Zion to be built and ranged from spiritualism to millennialism to socialist utopianism. The number of different religious options, many of which involved withdrawing from society and forming separate communities, was bewildering.

This urge to create separate communities was one of the more striking and distinctive features of the Second Great Awakening. Communitarianism could be found in several sections of the country, but mainly in isolated areas and near the frontier. Most of the communities disappeared almost as quickly as they surfaced, but one prominent and relatively lasting example was established by Ann Lee Stanley, or Mother Ann Lee, who migrated to the United States from Great Britain in the 1770s and settled in Albany, New York. She preached the duality of God, the masculine and feminine: Christ was the masculine expression of God's personality and, according to believers, Mother Ann was one of the feminine expressions. She also taught the sinfulness of sex and the necessity of celibacy. Her followers called themselves the United Society of Believers in Christ's Second Appearance but were generally known as Shakers on account of their dancing ritual, which involved the violent shaking of the body. Although

Mother Ann died in 1784, the numbers of Shakers grew steadily during the next several decades and their individual communities expanded to two dozen. The simplicity, grace, and beauty of their houses and furniture were so masterful that they produced a unique and lasting style of American design and craftsmanship that is still admired today.

Into this maelstrom of economic, political, intellectual, and religious turbulence Joseph Smith Jr., the Prophet, was born. Religious excitement was part of the very air he breathed. However, he was not simply molded by the events transpiring around him; he was also and most profoundly shaped by the powerful influence of his deeply religious parents and by his residence in the western frontier of New York in the heart of the Burned-Over District.

Joseph's mother, Lucy Mack, was the descendant of an immigrant from Inverness, Scotland, who came to this country in 1699 and settled in Salisbury, Massachusetts. Her family prospered and moved several times before her father, Solomon Mack, took up residence in Gilsum, New Hampshire, along the northern frontier. Solomon farmed, married Lydia Gates, a schoolteacher and steadfast member of the Congregational Church, and had eight children, the last of whom was Lucy, born on July 8, 1775.

The Mack family held strong religious beliefs, but a succession of family illnesses and deaths deeply depressed Lucy and made her "pensive and melancholy." First her father suffered a dreadful accident when a tree fell on him and nearly crippled him. A few years later, after his recovery, he left for Nova Scotia to run a coasting trade from Halifax to St. John. During his absence Lucy's mother, Lydia, contracted a severe illness and seemed so close to death that she called her children around her bed to say farewell and exhort them to "fear God and walk uprightly before Him." Then she asked her son Stephen to take the eight-year-old Lucy into his home and raise her as his own. Stephen was nine years older than his sister. Fortunately the mother recovered in six months and the daughter returned home.

When Lucy was fourteen her married sister Lovisa became deathly ill with tuberculosis and for three days lay in a comatose state. Then, suddenly, on the night of the third day at two o'clock in the morning, according to Lucy's account written decades later, Lovisa roused herself and cried out, "The Lord has healed me, soul and body. Raise me up and give me my clothes. I want to get up." Dressed, she was lifted from her bed and raised to the floor, but the weight of her body dislocated both feet. "Put me in a chair and pull my feet gently," she commanded, "and I shall soon be sound again." And so it happened, just as she instructed.

Lovisa's miraculous recovery had a profound effect on Lucy and on the community at large. Neighbors crowded into the house where Lovisa spoke to them, sang a hymn "with angelic harmony," and told them to meet with her on Thursday in the village church where she would relate in detail the circumstances of her recovery.

A large congregation dutifully jammed into the church to hear about the miracle. The minister yielded his pulpit to Lovisa so she could tell her story. She started by singing a hymn, after which she launched into a recital of her unique experience. "I seemed to be borne away to the world of spirits," she began, "where I saw the Savior as through a veil, which appeared to me about as thick as a spider's web, and he told me that I must return again to warn the people to prepare for death; that I must exhort them to be watchful as well as prayer-

ful . . . and that if I would do this my life would be pro-
longed." She ended her discourse with a lengthy commentary
on "the uncertainty of life."

Lovisa became a celebrity for the next several years. Her
house was always crowded with people and she did not hesi-
tate to speak at length about her "miraculous recovery" and
the visitation she had experienced. Echoes of these events
would later surface in Joseph Smith's life.

But her vision was not extraordinary. During the Second
Great Awakening many men and women—particularly adoles-
cents—claimed to have seen and talked with God the Father
and His Son, Jesus Christ. One young man, Billy Hibbard,
later wrote about a celestial experience he had had at the age of
eleven. And in 1815 Norris Stearns published a work describ-
ing his vision in which there suddenly appeared a "small gleam
of light in the room," brighter than the sun, and God the Cre-
ator and Christ the Redeemer stood before him. Lorenzo Dow
claimed that at the age of thirteen he was whisked to heaven by
a whirlwind and beheld a throne of ivory overlaid with gold,
with God sitting upon it attended by Christ at His right hand.

Following Lovisa's vision, another of Lucy's sisters, Lovina, developed an advanced case of tuberculosis and became
desperately ill. Lucy was obliged to assume the role of nurse to
the dying sister, tending to her every need. She fed her, washed
her, and carried her from the bed to a chair. Finally Lovina
asked Lucy to call the family together to hear her final farewell.
When they had gathered around her chair, she told them that
at the age of ten, "God . . . heard my prayers and forgave my
sins. Since then I have, according to my best ability, endeav-
ored to serve him continually. I have called you here to give
you my last warning and bid you all farewell and beseech you
to endeavor to meet me when parting shall be no more."

Lovina then asked Lucy to carry her back to her bed. Feeling her life draining away she called out to her parents, sisters, and brothers and bade them "all farewell. I am going to rest—prepare to follow me." Following that she sang a hymn, and when she finished she closed her eyes, folded her hands across her breast, and died.

The shock of Lovina's passing in 1794 was followed almost immediately by Lovisa's death, also of tuberculosis. Their demise so depressed the nineteen-year-old Lucy that she went to live again with her brother Stephen in Tunbridge, Vermont, in order, she later wrote, "to divert my mind from the death of my sister, as the grief of it was preying upon my health and was likely to be a serious injury to me." But her depression only deepened over the following months. So she turned to the Bible and "prayed incessantly." This only led to guilt feelings about not belonging to any particular church, and she worried that "all religious people will say I am of the world." Yet if she joined a particular church, "all the rest will say I am in error. No church will admit that I am right, except the one with which I am associated. This makes them witnesses against each other."

What to do? Which church to join? There was such a profusion of religious voices screaming their legitimacy that it was bewildering to an uneducated and inexperienced young woman. So she just continued praying and reading her Bible.

Lucy was a strong-minded, independent-thinking woman, committed to the belief that the inner religious experience dictated what a person should do, but her turn to religion was not unique in the family. Her oldest brother, Jason—he was fifteen years her senior—left home at an early age and became what was then called a "Seeker," believing that through prayer and faith he could attain the same "gifts of the Gospel" that were enjoyed by Christ's disciples. In 1780, at the age of twenty, he became a preacher of the Gospel. His was one of countless sects unaffiliated with any established church during the Second Great Awakening. He labored incessantly to convert others to his faith and was certain that God would "in the fulness of time" manifest His power "in signs and wonders." At his death he was practicing faith healing and holding daily meetings as he journeyed from town to town.

Lucy took great pride in Jason's accomplishments as a preacher and in his commitment to his unique religion. Although she herself could not find any Christian denomination that satisfied her religious needs, she kept hoping and praying. She remained a year with her brother Stephen in Tunbridge, where she met a tall, good-looking young man by the name of Joseph Smith, the father of the future Prophet. After a brief visit to her parents' home she was persuaded by her brother to return to Tunbridge. This time she remained with Stephen until she married Joseph Smith on January 24, 1796. She was now twenty and her husband twenty-four.

Smith's family had migrated from England in 1638 and settled in Topsfield, a small village eight miles north of Salem, Massachusetts. His father, Asael, was of the fourth generation in his family to live in the town. He married Mary Duty and later moved with his growing family to Windham, New Hampshire, where Mary's family lived, and then to Derryfield in 1778. He was elected town clerk, sired eleven children, and raised sheep and cattle for market. Then in June 1791 he purchased eighty-three acres of land in Tunbridge, Vermont, which his two eldest sons, Jesse and Joseph, helped him clear.

Asael, like Lucy Mack, had a strong sense of family. He told his children that he wanted them to "live together in an undivided bond of love." And when your parents are gone, he said, "be so many fathers and mothers to each other, so you shall understand the blessing mentioned in the 133 Psalm." Family was very important to the Smiths, and later an important component of the Mormon religion.

Unlike Solomon Mack, Asael Smith provided his children with a formal religious upbringing. They were baptized in the Congregational Church and taught to read the Bible diligently, to speak to God, to pray to Him, and to be earnest in addressing His "great majesty." Joseph, Asael's second son, imbibed this religiosity but, like his future wife, chose not to join any particular church. He remained steadfastly aloof from "conventional religion."

Asael became well acquainted with Stephen Mack in Tunbridge and quite intimate, even though twenty-two years separated the ages of the two men. Indeed, Stephen spoke of the Smiths as "worthy, respectable, amiable and intelligent." Through this connection Lucy met Joseph, and when they married, Asael presented his son with part ownership of a "handsome farm" while Stephen and his partner John Mudget gave Lucy a check of one thousand dollars. The young bride set the check aside because, she said, she had sufficient means of her own to purchase the necessary household furniture.

For the next six years the newlyweds farmed and produced two children: Alvin, born in 1798, and Hyrum, born in 1800. (Their first son, unnamed, died in childbirth.) Then in 1802 they rented their homestead and moved seven miles west to Randolph, where they opened a "mercantile establishment." They had hardly settled into their new home and opened their store when Lucy was taken ill with a severe cold. Fever set in and it was believed that, like her sisters before her, she had contracted tuberculosis. Her mother watched over her during her illness and cared for her. She appeared close to death when a Methodist minister came to visit. He seemed anxious to ask the patient whether she was prepared to die. It was a question Lucy feared to hear because "I did not consider myself ready for such an awful event, inasmuch as I knew not the ways of Christ; besides, there appeared to be a dark and lonesome chasm, between myself and the Savior, which I dared not attempt to pass."

While she meditated on death and her own unpreparedness for eternity, the minister left. A few moments later her husband entered the room quietly and took her by the hand. "O, Lucy!" he cried, "my wife! my wife! you must die! The doctors have given you up; and all say you can not live."

With that, Lucy turned to the Lord. She "begged and pleaded" that her life be spared so that she might raise her children and be a comfort to her husband. "My mind was much agitated during the whole night," she later recorded. Sometimes she contemplated heaven and the world to come. At other times she thought of her babies and her life companion and what might happen to them when she departed this life.

In her feverish state and sense of fear and longing, she decided to make "a solemn covenant with God": that if He allowed her to live she would endeavor to serve Him to the best of her ability for the rest of her life.

Suddenly, she later wrote, a voice responded. "Seek, and ye shall find; knock, and it shall be opened unto you. Let your heart be comforted; ye believe in God, believe also in me." In that moment, she said, she found peace. A few seconds later her mother entered the room and looked at what must have been Lucy's glowing face. "Lucy," she exclaimed, "you are better."

"Yes, mother," the young woman replied quietly, "the Lord will let me live, if I am faithful to the promise which I made to him, to be a comfort to my mother, my husband, and my children." Her mother broke down in tears. Praise God, she cried. Give Him thanks. "The Lord has done a marvelous work; let his name have the praise thereof."

Lucy had passed a crisis, and in succeeding days she continued to gain strength. Yet while her physical health improved, her mental outlook was deeply disturbed. "My mind was considerably disquieted," she admitted. "It was wholly occupied upon the subject of religion." She feared for her salvation and knew that she needed instruction in "the ways of Christ." A strong-minded woman, she determined to get completely well so she could find someone who could help her perfect her "way of life" and find salvation. She had made a covenant with the Lord and she fully intended to keep it.

She attended several Methodist revival meetings that had begun to appear in the community but finally decided there was not a religion on earth which could satisfy her yearning. So she made up her mind to dismiss all the denominations in her neighborhood and take Jesus and His disciples as her teachers and the Bible as her guide to life and salvation.

For Lucy, God had become a ubiquitous presence with whom she communicated freely and frequently. Her God virtually became a member of the family who not only spoke to her but invaded her dreams and cured her illnesses and those of her loved ones. So for the next several years, she persisted in her regime of prayer and Bible reading and mystical experiences without bothering to join a particular church. But baptism seemed essential to her, so she found a minister who was willing to administer the rites without any obligation of joining his congregation.

Her husband, Joseph, also resisted committing himself to any one form of Christian worship. Since the Methodist revival meetings had attracted Lucy, Joseph obliged her by accompanying her. But his Congregationalist family ridiculed his attendance. Embarrassed, he told his wife that the meetings had little value and only wasted their time. He took the position that no one sect knew more about the Kingdom of God than any other. As for himself, he would simply abide by "the ancient order, as established by our Lord and Savior Jesus Christ, and his Apostles." He continued relying on the Bible and on the various forms of folk magic he regularly practiced. As a believer in the supernatural he accepted the existence of witches and demons as readily as that of angels and prophets. He regularly used divining rods and seerstones to discover unseen treasures and unravel mysteries. The presence of water, for example, could be found by using a forked stick or hazel rod. Joseph also believed he could uncover hidden treasure with witch hazel. He would hold a fork in each hand as he hunted for these unseen riches. He claimed the "upper end was attracted by the money."

Of even greater use to believers were the seerstones. These were stones of various sizes and colors through which one could look to see what was hidden from normal sight. Some of the stones were greenish, others white like marble. Some had holes in the middle so they could also be worn as amulets. A seer would place the stone in a hat, bury his face in the hat, and see things that were invisible to the naked eye.

Joseph used seerstones to treasure-hunt, and Lucy, and later his sons, helped him in the practice. But the Smiths were not the only ones. The *Palmyra Herald* of July 24, 1822, reported in an article entitled "Money Diggers" that "at least five hundred respectable men . . . verily believe that immense treasures lie concealed upon our Green Mountains; many of whom have been for a number of years, most industriously and perseveringly engaged in digging it up. Some of them have succeeded beyond their most sanguine expectations."

For Joseph treasure digging became a regular summertime activity along with farming and running his store. But he failed miserably in everything he tried. He invested heavily in ginseng for the China trade, but an agent absconded with the profits, leaving Joseph penniless. He was forced to sell the farm he had inherited for $800 and use Lucy's dowry to pay off outstanding debts to Boston merchants. Landless, the family moved seven times over a period of fourteen years. Between 1803, the year their first daughter, Sophronia, was born, and 1811 they circled around Tunbridge, Royalton, and Sharon, renting one farm after another in a desperate search for better economic opportunities.

Their families helped them in their plight, and they never starved. Joseph taught school in Sharon during the winter and farmed and dug for treasure in the summer. They were living in Sharon when their third son was born on December 23, 1805. He was named after his father and would soon demonstrate extraordinary talents. Joseph Smith Jr. arrived into a family of religious zealots at a time and place drenched in religious fervor, if not frenzy, with practices of divination, magic, astrology, alchemy, and mysticism commonplace occurrences.

Fourteen years later he had his first vision.

Chapter 2

First Vision

At the time of Joseph Jr.'s birth, Thomas Jefferson had begun his second term as president of the United States. The recent purchase of Louisiana from France in 1803 raised his popularity to new heights. This enormous expanse of territory, virtually doubling the geographical extent of the country, opened up the possibility of claiming the entire Pacific Northwest, particularly after Lewis and Clark explored the Columbia River to the Pacific Ocean in 1805 in what are now the states of Oregon and Washington. Jefferson wrongly surmised that this new territory would provide land for Americans for a thousand generations.

Actually Americans had already begun their steady march westward. After scaling the Allegheny Mountains they settled into the lush valleys of the Ohio, Tennessee, and Mississippi Rivers, ousting Native Americans as they went and establishing democratic local governments. By the end of the eighteenth century Kentucky and Tennessee had entered the Union, followed in the next two decades by eight additional states. When Missouri (the twenty-fourth state) was admitted as part of the Missouri Compromise of 1820–1821, it was the first state lying totally west of the Mississippi River.

President Jefferson's initial term in office had been blessed with a series of political and economic triumphs, but his second term verged on disaster. In 1805 the United States found itself caught between two warring powers, England and France,

18

who regularly violated American neutrality by seizing U.S. ships and, in the case of Britain, impressing American seamen. When a British man-of-war captured the American frigate *Chesapeake* and hauled it off to Halifax, Congress passed the Embargo Act prohibiting all imports and exports into or out of American seaports. Jefferson desperately tried to maintain the country's neutrality but it was becoming impossible. His successor, James Madison, faced an outraged Congress, led by War Hawks like Henry Clay and John C. Calhoun, among others, who demanded that he ask Congress for a declaration of war in order to end the humiliation and hardships the nation had been forced to endure. Madison finally acquiesced, and in June 1812 the United States declared war against Great Britain, a war which brought repeated military disasters, including the capture and burning of Washington and the blockade of virtually the entire eastern coastline.

Joseph and Lucy Smith also suffered during this turbulent period as they kept up a frantic search for a better life. The arrival of several more children—Samuel (1808), Ephraim (1810), William (1811), and Catherine (1813)—only intensified their poverty. But immersed as they were in the revivalist tumult of the age, they had faith that the Lord would assist them in their search. Not surprisingly, it was at this time that Joseph Smith Sr. had a religious experience of profound importance. Lucy said that her husband's mind had recently become "much excited upon the subject of religion." He went to bed one night while "contemplating the situation of the Christian religion, or the confusion and discord that were extant," and had an extraordinary dream. It seems he was walking in a wide, open, and barren field and saw nothing but dead and fallen trees. Silence prevailed in this gloomy desert. "An attendant spirit" accompanying Joseph told him that the field was the world, which lay "inanimate and dumb, in regard to the true religion, or plan of salvation." The spirit then instructed him to walk on where he would find a box on a log, "the contents of which, if you eat thereof, will make you wise." Joseph found the box and when he opened it "all manner of beasts, horned cattle, and roaring animals, rose up on every side in the most threatening manner possible, tearing the earth, tossing their horns, and bellowing most terrifically" around him. Joseph dropped the box and ran for his life. Yet, strangely, in the midst of all this, "I was perfectly happy," he told Lucy, "though I awoke trembling."

This was the first of seven dreams or visions, as Lucy called them, that Joseph Smith Sr. experienced between 1811 and 1819. The appearance of a spirit messenger in dreams was not uncommon in folk magic at this time and the presence of a box that could make one wise would later play a significant role in his son's encounter with the supernatural. Revivalists at the time preached that dreams were inspired by God. But Joseph Sr.'s visions apparently confirmed his belief that all churches knew no more about the Kingdom of God than any layman.

As deeply religious parents, Joseph and Lucy Smith related these dreams to their children, who surely were profoundly affected by them, especially the very impressionable Joseph Jr. Moreover, the children were subjected to regular religious sessions in which they all prayed, sang hymns, and listened to prayers as their parents beseeched the Almighty to save their children from sin. The parents confessed their own transgressions and poured out their needs and fears to the Lord. These religious sessions, William Smith later reported, took place morning and night, and were an integral part of Smith family life, as they undoubtedly were among many other families drenched in the religious fervor of the age.

Lucy was particularly zealous in the religious upbringing of her children. "A very pious woman," much concerned about the welfare of her children, "both here and hereafter," according to her son, she "made use of every means which her parental love could suggest to get us engaged in seeking for our soul's salvation." And she succeeded beyond every expectation.

In 1811 the family moved from Vermont to Lebanon, New Hampshire, and here the Smiths markedly improved their financial status and sent their oldest children to school. Alvin at age thirteen and Sophronia, eight, attended a public school in Lebanon, while Hyrum, eleven, was sent to Moor's Charity School, which was associated with Dartmouth College in Hanover. The youngest children, Joseph Jr., five, Samuel, three, and William, six months, stayed home.

Lke all schoolchildren, Sophronia, Hyrum, and Alvin contracted a variety of illnesses. Unfortunately, one of these was typhoid fever, which had swept through the Connecticut River valley leaving thousands dead. It hit Lebanon with devastating force and infected several of the Smith children.

Sophronia was the worst off. She came down with the fever, and after ninety days a physician pronounced her condition hopeless. The child lay on her bed motionless; she seemed near death. The parents sank to their knees alongside the bed, clasped hands "and poured out our grief to God, in prayer and supplication, beseeching him to spare our child yet a little longer."

And the Lord heard their petition, Lucy later reported. Sophronia appeared to have stopped breathing, so the mother wrapped the child in a blanket, took her in her arms, and paced the floor. Lucy had faith that God in His mercy had the "power to save to the uttermost all who call on Him." And at length, she said, He responded. As Lucy pressed Sophronia to her breast the child sobbed. Then again. Finally Sophronia looked up at her mother and started breathing normally. "My soul was satisfied," Lucy exulted. "I laid my daughter on the bed, and sank by her side, completely overpowered by the intensity of my feelings."

The five-year-old Joseph Jr. also contracted the disease. But he apparently recovered after two weeks. Then one day while sitting in a chair he felt a sharp pain in his shoulder and let out a scream. He writhed in agony and his frightened parents hurriedly summoned a physician. After examining the child, Dr. Parker said he believed the pain had been caused by a sprain. But the boy protested that he had suffered no injury. Besides, the pain had come upon him suddenly when he was practically motionless.

The doctor dismissed the protest and applied a "bone linament" to the shoulder and "the hot shovel." They had no effect. Weeks of "extreme suffering" passed before the doctor deigned to take a closer look. On further examination he spotted a large fever sore in the child's armpit. He lanced it, whereupon it discharged a quart of "purulent matter."

The pain subsided momentarily. But then it "shot like lightening" down his left side into the marrow of the bone of his left leg "& terminated in a fever sore of the worst kind." Joseph cried out, "Oh, father! the pain is so severe, how can I bear it." The leg swelled and for the next two weeks the boy suffered in agony. Lucy carried him in her arms to assuage the pain, but nothing helped. His brother Hyrum sat beside him almost day and night, holding Joseph's leg and squeezing it between his hands to help him endure the excruciating torment. After three weeks of this torture the family summoned Dr. Stone, a surgeon, who made an eight-inch incision on the front side of the left leg between the knee and ankle—and without anesthesia. But it did relieve the pain once the initial discomfort of the operation subsided.

Unfortunately, in the following days and weeks infection set in and the leg swelled again and revived the pain. When the swelling grew worse the parents decided to call in a "council of surgeons." As it turned out, these surgeons were among the most distinguished physicians in New England. They included Dr. Nathan Smith, founder of the Dartmouth Medical School, and Dr. Cyrus Perkins, a trustee of the college, along with a number of medical students. The boy had apparently contracted osteomyelitis, usually a bacterial infection of the bone and bone marrow that causes high fever, chills, pain, and an abscess at the infection site. Without modern antibiotics there was no way to prevent bone destruction. So, after examining the boy, the surgeons left to consult among themselves.

What happened next to the five-year-old Joseph Smith Jr. provides a pretty heroic picture of a very young child. Mormons will most likely believe every word of it; non-Mormons will be understandably skeptical. What should be remembered is that this account was written more than thirty years later by a sixty-nine-year-old mother after her son had established the Mormon Church and been recognized by thousands of converts as a Prophet of God, and after he had been assassinated. That is not to accuse her of lying or deliberately misrepresenting the facts. As a strong, proud, deeply religious woman caught up in the revivalist fervor of her time, she probably remembered the incident exactly as she described it. No doubt what she said was very real to her. But her narrative must be weighed against reasonable expectations of the mental and emotional capacity of a five-year-old.

As Joseph himself later remembered it, eleven doctors

came to amputate his leg. As they entered the house Lucy pleadingly asked, "Gentlemen, what can you do to save my boy's leg?" The answer must have hit her with devastating force. The council of surgeons recommended amputation. "We can do nothing," they answered her; "we have cut it open to the bone, and find it so affected that we consider the leg incurable, and that amputation is absolutely necessary in order to save his life."

It was like a "thunder bolt," Lucy admitted. But she refused to accept the verdict. "Can you not, by cutting around the bone, take out the diseased part, and perhaps that which is sound will heal over, and by this means you will save his leg?" Understand me, she continued in as forceful a manner as she knew how, "You will not, you must not, take off his leg, until you try once more. I will not consent to let you enter his room until you make me this promise."

The doctors huddled for a consultation. After a brief pause they turned to Lucy and gave their solemn word to do what she had requested. They then entered young Joseph's room, and one of the doctors walked over to the patient's bed and said, "My poor boy, we have come again."

"Yes," the child responded, "I see you have; but you have not come to take off my leg, have you, sir?" Joseph later remembered that he "utterly refused to give my assent to the operation."

"No," replied the doctor, "it is your mother's request that we make one more effort, and that is what we have come for."

Since it would be an excruciating procedure without anesthesia the doctor called for ropes to bind the child to the bedstead.

According to Lucy, her son refused to be tied down. "No,

doctor," he said, "I will not be bound, for I can bear the operation much better if I have my liberty."

"Then," the doctor asked, "will you drink some brandy?"

"No," answered the boy, "not one drop."

"Will you take some wine? You must take something, or you can never endure the severe operation to which you must be subjected."

"No," insisted Joseph, "I will not touch one particle of liquor, neither will I be tied down; but I will tell you what I will do—I will have my father sit on the bed and hold me in his arms, and then I will do whatever is necessary in order to have the bone taken out." Turning to his mother, he continued, "Mother, I want you to leave the room, for I know you can not bear to see me suffer so; father can stand it, but you have carried me so much, and watched over me so long, you are almost worn out."

With tears in his eyes he looked intently into Lucy's face. "Now, mother, promise me that you will not stay, will you? The Lord will help me, and I shall get through with it."

Lucy left the room and the doctors commenced the operation. They drilled into one side of the bone and then on the other side, using whatever primitive surgical instruments were available. After that they broke off the first piece of diseased bone with forceps. When they did Joseph screamed so loudly that his mother raced back into the room to console and help her son. But, again, the child ordered her away.

When a third piece was removed Lucy burst into the room once more. "And oh, my God!" she wrote, "what a spectacle for a mother's eye." There was a gaping wound with blood still rushing from it; the bed was soaked with blood, and Joseph lay pale as a corpse, his face a portrait of "the utmost agony."

Lucy was forcibly removed from the room and possibly restrained until the operation concluded. When the doctors finally finished what must have been a grueling task they carried away all signs of the operation and every trace of blood. They laid the boy on a clean bed and he began a long period of recovery. The fact that he survived this trauma at all seems miraculous. He was just fortunate to have come under the knife of some of the most skilled surgeons in New England. Dr. Nathan Smith had treated such cases before and had developed a surgical procedure to deal with it that was far in advance of his time.

The next several months were a torment for Joseph and his family as the leg slowly healed. Over the course of that time some fourteen pieces of bone worked their way to the surface and were expelled. During these agonizing days Joseph was carried about by his mother. Later he used crutches to move around the house and farm. When he had recovered sufficiently to travel he was sent to the home of his uncle Jesse Smith in Salem, Massachusetts, to improve his health. It was hoped that the sea breezes would prove beneficial, and indeed they did. But for the remainder of his life Joseph Smith Jr. walked with a slight limp. What emotional and psychological scars he carried into adulthood is impossible to state with certainty. But surely the illness, the excruciating pain he suffered for months, and the limp he developed must have had a tremendous psychological impact on him and on the kind of person he became. It is entirely possible that it conditioned him for the career he chose and the suffering and persecution he later endured. It may even have focused his attention more sharply on the afterlife.

Other than his operation and recovery there is not much known about Joseph's early life. A full year passed before his health and that of the other members of the Smith family were restored, but the expense and anguish took their toll on each one of them. The boy did not receive much formal education at this time, but his father, having once taught school, quite probably instructed him. Naturally, Joseph Jr. read his Bible regularly, and he later said he thought deeply about it.

With the family's resources dwindling, the thought arose that the Smiths should pull up stakes in New Hampshire and start afresh back in Vermont. In 1814 they recrossed the Connecticut River and settled in Norwich, Vermont, about eight or nine miles from their former home, and rented a farm from Squire Moredock.

Meanwhile the War of 1812 ended when American commissioners signed a treaty of peace with the British in Ghent, Belgium, on Christmas Eve 1814. Two weeks later Major General Andrew Jackson and his army destroyed a British invading force intent on capturing and looting New Orleans, a victory that generated a spirit of nationalism throughout the country and elevated Jackson to the rank of national hero. Three years later, in 1818, he added to his heroic stature when, at the direction of the administration of President James Monroe, he invaded Spanish Florida (presumably on a mission to subdue the Seminole Indians, who had attacked the Georgia and Alabama frontiers) and seized the colony from Spain. After protracted negotiations Spain agreed to sell Florida to the United States for five million dollars in debts owed to American citizens. It also relinquished to this country its claim to the entire Pacific Northwest.

As the nation grew in size and population, so too did the Smith family, and their resources were stretched to the limit. For three years, during the births of Catherine in 1813 and Don Carlos in 1816, one crop failure followed another. They survived by selling fruit that grew on the farm and working at whatever jobs they could find in town. Lucy helped out by painting oilcloth coverings for tables and stands. A climactic end to their existence in Norwich came in 1816, the so-called year without a summer. Freakish weather produced several inches of snow on June 8 and froze over small ponds. The disastrous crop failure for the third year in a row—it almost caused a famine, said Lucy—convinced a great many Vermonters to pack up and head west. Over the next two years, thousands of families took off. A migration began from which Vermont did not recover for nearly a century.

What to do? Joseph Smith Sr. came home one day, said Lucy, sat down, and meditated. His meditation lasted several hours. Then suddenly he roused himself and announced to his family that he had decided to move to New York in the company of a Mr. Howard who was going to the upstate town of Palmyra. Smith's brothers and father had already relocated in northern New York, which added to the attractiveness of the place. He informed his family that he would precede them to Palmyra and prepare the way. Meanwhile Lucy, her mother, who had been living with the family, and the older boys would begin collecting and packing their belongings in preparation for their departure.

So off Joseph Sr. went, and not much later he sent his family a wagon and a team of horses with Caleb Howard, a cousin of his traveling companion, to serve as guide. But at the last minute creditors showed up and threatened legal action if Lucy did not pay their claims before leaving. Rather than delay her departure or fight the claims in court, she agreed to their demands. "By making considerable exertion," she wrote, "I raised the required sum, which was one hundred and fifty dollars, and liquidated the demand."

It was a cold, snowy day in 1816 when Lucy and her brood of eight children—Alvin, eighteen; Hyrum, sixteen; Sophronia, thirteen; Joseph Jr., ten; Samuel, eight; William, five; Catherine, three; and Don Carlos, eight months—left Norwich. They stopped at Royalton to leave Lucy's mother with her brother Daniel Mack. As they continued their journey they were joined by a Mr. Gates and his family who were also headed west. However, Caleb Howard, their teamster, proved to be an "unprincipled and unfeeling wretch," declared Lucy, who forced Joseph Jr. to walk miles each day through the snow, despite his lameness. Young Joseph later remembered suffering "the most excruciating weariness & pain, & all this that Mr Howard might enjoy the society of Mr Gates' Daughters which he took on the waggon where I should have Rode." When Alvin and Hyrum protested, Howard knocked them down with the butt of his whip.

Upon arriving in Utica, New York, the teamster tossed the Smiths' household goods out of the wagon and prepared to run off with the rig. But Lucy seized the reins and called on bystanders to witness that she was being robbed of a wagon and goods that belonged to her husband, leaving her destitute with eight children and no means of continuing her journey. Then, turning to Howard, she screamed: "You can go about your own business; I shall take charge of the team myself, and hereafter attend to my own business."

And she did. But she left young Joseph behind to ride on one of the Gateses' sleighs. Then, as the boy attempted to take his place on the sleigh, one of the Gates sons, who was the driver, knocked him down and he was left, he said, "to wallow in my blood until a stranger came along, picked me up, & carried me to the Town of Palmyra."

It should be noted here that Joseph's early history, as told by him and his disciples, involved repeated hostility by any number of people he met, even those who barely knew him. Was the purpose of the stories to indicate how he was being prepared for the anger and hatred he would endure once he revealed his encounters with the divine?

With the rest of her family in tow, poor Lucy drove on wearily and paid for lodging and food with "bits of cloth, clothing . . . and the drops [earrings]" belonging to Sophronia. The journey had taken them almost a month over snow-covered terrain, but they arrived safely in Palmyra. When she greeted her husband all she had left was "barely two cents in cash." Still they were safe and now reunited and they could begin a new life in a thriving town just north of the Finger Lakes. They arrived right smack in the heart of the Burned-Over District.

Palmyra in 1816 was a good-size town of about four thousand, even though it had been settled only twenty-five years earlier. And Canandaigua, a dozen miles to the south, was even bigger. In and near the two towns there were schools, libraries, female seminaries, seventy-six shops, paved sidewalks, three churches, and enough revival meetings to satisfy even the most heaven-bent of Christian worshipers. Palmyra sat on the proposed site of the Erie Canal, a stupendous undertaking that Governor DeWitt Clinton had just persuaded the New York legislature to begin. When completed in 1825 this 363-mile stretch of waterway would ultimately link the harbor of New York City with the Great Lakes and cause land prices to skyrocket along its route.

For a year and a half the Smith family lived in Palmyra on rented land, paid for by the father and sons, who hired out digging wells, haying, and harvesting, and by Lucy, who painted oilcloths. She also opened a small "cake and beer shop" and sold boiled eggs, gingerbread, and root beer. They ultimately built a log house on a farm in what became the town of Manchester. In time this community boasted a school, a library, a woolen mill, a flour mill, a paper mill, and a blast furnace. At this point in their lives, according to Lucy, the family was "living comfortably." We "blessed God, with our whole heart, for his 'mercy which endureth for ever.' And not only temporal blessings were bestowed upon us, but also spiritual were administered."

Young Joseph grew stronger and more self-reliant as he progressed into his teenage years. Tall for his age, with light-colored hair and a bright, engaging smile, he made a striking appearance even at a young age. His mother said he was "remarkably quiet," a "well-disposed child," and "always seemed to reflect more deeply than common persons of his age upon everything of a religious nature." He was much "given to reflection and deep study," which she took as a sure sign of his developing interest in the things of God. In addition he was highly emotional and would break down in tears at the slightest provocation. Entering puberty is a trial for any teenager; fortunately, Joseph had powerful parental direction. His strong-willed mother was a particularly commanding influence on his development, especially on his religious convictions and moral outlook. She frequently related to him the experiences of her family and her own visions of and commitment to the Lord. The impact of her convictions, her sense of the real presence of God in her life, along with the religious ambience of the Second Great Awakening in this Burned-Over District, helped mold Joseph Jr. and point him in the extraordinary direction his life took over the next few years.

Not that Joseph Sr. was without influence. Indeed, in some ways, his influence was even more pronounced. He continued to have dreams or visions, which he related to his wife, who later included them in her history of the family. Joseph heard them as well. Most of these dreams had similar characteristics. He was usually ill or lame but had a guide attending him to provide directions. Invariably he was on a desolate plain or a gloomy desert shrouded in utter silence. He always seemed bent on achieving some ill-defined goal (salvation?) that lay beyond him.

At the age of twelve, Joseph later admitted, his "mind became seriously imprest with regard to the all important concerns for the wellfare of my immortal soul which led me to searching the scriptures believing as I was taught, that they contained the word of God." He continued to dwell on these thoughts and dutifully read the Bible as each night and day the family gathered for prayers, hymns, and the confession of sins.

Such was the Smith household during Joseph Jr.'s early life. But the father's influence involved outdoor activities as well. Not only did he train his boys in the skills of husbandry but he brought with him the folklore of "money digging" with its spells and incantations. In Palmyra he resumed his search for treasure and introduced young Joseph to the occult. A Palmyra newspaper reported that many men and women, particularly those "unchurched" who practiced folk religion, "became marvellous wise in the occult sciences." They had dreams and visions which disclosed treasures hidden deep in the earth. Divining rods, an occult tool, were generally the instrument of choice, said the newspaper. They were supposedly "infallible guides to these sources of wealth." Since crystal gazing was an old and honored practice, peepstones or seerstones gathered from the "brook or field" were also part of the folk magic of the early nineteenth century. The stone would be placed in a hat to exclude light, the newspaper report continued, whereupon persons, male or female, "applied their eyes, and . . . declared they saw the wonders of nature, including of course, ample stores of silver and gold." Most probably, claims one Mormon historian, young Joseph began following his father's example in using divining rods and seerstones between age eleven and thirteen. A friendly neighbor of the Smiths declared that both father and son "believed in witchcraft." The witch hazel stick and mineral rod, together with spells and magic incantations, aided them in their hunt. They were repeatedly seen poking around the ground, for there were many Indian burial mounds in the Palmyra area filled with artifacts made of copper, stone, and sometimes silver. Who knows, there might even be Spanish bullion to be found. As he grew, Joseph became quite skilled in this activity and developed a reputation as an intrepid money digger.

One neighbor recalled that young Joseph boasted that a chest full of gold watches was buried on his property and that he gathered a group of friends to help him dig for it. To start, they drove stakes into the ground in a circle over the selected spot and one member of the team marched around the circle with a weapon to "guard against any assault which his Satanic majesty might be disposed to make" while the others dug for the treasure. Unfortunately they found nothing and the site was abandoned.

Young Joseph used seerstones as well. Various sources declared that he had three such stones: his first was obtained by digging it out of the ground after he had seen it when using a neighbor's stone; the second was a gift; and the third he and his brother Alvin uncovered while digging a well. It was this third seerstone that Joseph Jr. used most extensively. With it, his mother said, he could see things "invisible to natural eye." It was small and rather dark in color with light-colored stripes and a shape like a hen's egg. Isaac Hale, Joseph's future father-in-law, and other neighbors testified that Joseph would place the "stone . . . in his hat, and his hat closed over his face," to exclude all light save what emanated from the stone itself. In such manner he was able "to see all things within and under the earth." Joseph later said that "every man who lived on the earth was entitled to a seerstone and should have one, but they are kept from them in consequence of their wickedness."

It is possible that because Joseph became so adept at treasure digging someone, perhaps in a fit of jealousy, tried to kill him. The attempt allegedly occurred one evening when the fourteen-year-old boy was returning home from an errand. Suddenly a shot rang out as he passed through the dooryard. Luckily it missed him. Frightened, he rushed into the house to escape. But who would do such a thing? The following day the family found a dead cow with bullets in its head and neck; the cow had been standing in a dark corner. They never discovered the person who tried to kill Joseph, if in fact that was his purpose, or what possible reason he might have to harm him. But this, if true, was the first of many attempts on his life.

In view of his unpleasant experiences during his journey from Norwich, Vermont, to Palmyra, this incident clearly demonstrated another example of the animosity and hatred he could arouse in others. Something about him provoked a certain type of person, even at this early age. His arrogance? His boasting? His need to control and direct other people? Whatever it was, this hostility from others and their desire to do him harm would remain a persistent theme throughout his life. Hostile skeptics, however, dismiss the story as pure myth, concocted like the other incidents of enmity out of trivial incidents and inserted into the hagiography of Joseph's life so as to foreshadow his actual persecution and death.

Around this time Joseph Sr. experienced a renewal of his visions. Most probably they occurred because Palmyra had become swamped with evangelicals holding camp meetings. "There was a great revival in religion" at the time, declared Lucy, to which Joseph Jr. added that there was "unusual excitement on the subject of religion. It commenced with the Methodists but soon became general among all the sects in that region of the country." The preaching by these sects was usually very animated, the responses quite frenzied. This was particularly true at the camp meetings when men and women would shout their repentance. "Hysterical sobbings, convulsive groans, shrieks and screams the most appalling" were not uncommon during these services. "Oh, woe! woe!" wept one woman at a particularly lively gathering. "When I was fifteen my mother died, and I backslided, oh Jesus, I backslided! take me home to my mother, Jesus! take me home to her, for I am weary! Hear it, hear it, Jesus."

"Amen! Amen!" responded another. "Jesus! Jesus! Glory! Glory!"

"Sister! dear sister!" the preacher cried. "This night was fixed upon for anxious sinners to wrestle with the Lord." Come, all of you, repent, fall on your knees and pray.

The crowd sprawled on the ground "in an indescribable confusion of heads and legs. They threw about their limbs with such incessant and violent motion" that it was a miracle no one was seriously hurt.

Small wonder the senior Smith had a renewal of his dreams or visions at this time. And the impact such wild scenes had upon someone as emotional and receptive as the younger Smith can well be imagined. To those who were unaccustomed to seeing men and women convulsively twisting and contorting and screaming, the sight must have come as quite a shock. "I felt sick with horror," wrote one observer. It was reminiscent of a scene in hell described by Dante in his *Inferno*, she added.

Prophets who called believers to come together and follow them regularly appeared in the Burned-Over District. Isaac Bullard, who preached free love and a communitarian society, gathered his disciples at Woodstock, Vermont, and marched them through New York, following the same route taken by the Smiths, and then moved on into Ohio and finally Missouri. He pronounced bathing a sin and claimed he had not changed his clothes in seven years.

Jemima Wilkinson claimed she was Christ and governed her congregation by revelations from God. She convinced her followers that she would never die. Both Jemima's group and the Shakers practiced rites that involved intensely physical manifestations. The Shakers became so well known for their "dancing" that people paid to watch them spin, whirl, and gallop.

Frances Trollope, a visitor from England who attended these extraordinary and violent exhibitions of religious faith, asked the meaning of a revival and was told that it involved "an elegant kindling of the spirit; it is brought about to the Lord's people by the hands of his saints, and it means salvation in the highest."

Salvation was what members of the Smith family desperately wanted, and they responded to these revivals in different ways. After sampling one sect after another, Lucy finally overcame her prejudice against established churches and joined the Western Presbyterian Church in Palmyra, along with her sons Hyrum and Samuel and her daughter Sophronia. But the two Josephs in the family remained aloof from organized religion, not that they eschewed it totally. Young Joseph leaned toward

Methodism, which held one of its greatest revival meetings at that time, and he "confessed some desire" to join that church. After catching a "spark" from a Methodist camp meeting, he became a "passable exhorter." He said he "wanted to get religion too, wanted to feel and shout like the rest." Unfortunately he "could feel nothing."

So young Joseph kept searching. "From the age of twelve years to fifteen," he later declared, "I pondered many things in my heart concerning the situation of the world of mankind . . . [and] the welfare of my immortal soul." Oppressed by his own sinfulness, he yearned for salvation. He wanted desperately to join a church but could not decide which one to embrace. People, he said, cried out, "lo, here!" and others, "lo, there." Methodists contended against Presbyterians and both against Baptists. They used all their skills and "sophistry" to prove the errors in one another. In this "war of words and tumult of opinions," Joseph asked himself: Which one is right? And how can I know it? Or were they all wrong?

It was while depressed by these thoughts and anxieties that Joseph turned to the scriptures for help, as he had been taught. He began to read the epistle of the Apostle James, first chapter, fifth verse: "*If any of you lack wisdom,*" he read, "*let him ask of God, that giveth to all men liberally, and upbraideth not; and it shall be given him.*"

The passage hit him like a thunderbolt. Surely if that passage applied to anyone, he thought, it applied to himself. He said it penetrated his very being with "great force" and into every "feeling of my heart." He realized in an instant that he must either remain "in darkness and confusion" or heed the words of the apostle. So this fourteen-year-old boy retired to the woods where he could be away from his family and the familiar surroundings of his home. He went where it was quiet and peaceful, where he could speak directly to God and ask for His help.

It was a beautiful clear day, he later remembered. He looked around to be sure he was alone. Then he knelt and "offered up the desires of my heart to God." He had scarcely formed the thought and words when he was seized by some power that "entirely overcame me" and bound his tongue so that he could not speak. Thick darkness closed in on him. At that moment, he said, it seemed as if he was "doomed to sudden destruction." In his mind and heart he cried out to God to save him and deliver him from the power of this enemy. He was about to sink into total despair and abandon himself to "destruction" when, he later claimed, a pillar of light above his head shone down and gradually descended until it fell directly on him. No sooner did this brilliant light appear than Joseph was delivered from the enemy and he saw two "Personages" whose "brightness and glory defy all description." They stood above him in the light "and exactly resembled each other in features and likeness."

"One of them spake unto me, calling me by name and said, pointing to the other: *This is My Beloved Son. Hear Him!*"

Finding his power of speech restored, Joseph responded by asking the question that had plagued him constantly: Which church was right? Which sect should he join?

The Personage told him that he "must join none of them." All the creeds of these sects "were an abomination in his sight." Their preachers were all corrupt and "they draw near me with their lips but their hearts are far from me, they teach for doctrines the commandments of man, having a form of godliness, but they deny the power thereof." Again the Personage warned Joseph against joining any of these churches.

When he finally came back to full consciousness the boy

found himself lying on his back looking up to heaven. The light had departed and he had little strength. After a few minutes he was able to get up and walk home. His mother looked at him and asked what was wrong. He dismissed her question by telling her that he was fine. But he also said that he had "learned that Presbyterianism is not true."

Joseph's experience in 1820 is known today by Mormons as the First Vision: first because it was the start of a series of revelations that marks for them, as one Mormon historian has written, the beginning of the restoration of the Gospel and the commencement of a new dispensation. Not that Joseph realized these implications at the time. His full understanding of what had happened to him came later.

Chapter 3

Moroni

THE BOY DID NOT TELL his parents about the vision. But a few days later he happened to be in the company of one of the Methodist preachers who were very active in the religious excitement engulfing Palmyra and told him of his experience. The clergyman, Joseph later reported, was aghast at what he was told and treated the story with contempt. He said that there were no such things as visions or revelations, that they no longer happened, that they ended with the Apostles. It was all the work of the devil and Joseph had better watch out because he might imperil his immortal soul.

Actually, reports of visions and divine appearances were commonplace at the time. And the fact that the boy had just turned fourteen should not have caused the preacher to summarily reject Joseph's story, since children were constantly reporting miraculous visitations. But what was objectionable to the preacher was the message, namely that all the churches were wrong and an abomination in God's sight. No preacher of an established church was about to accept that indictment. No wonder he called Joseph's vision a fraud.

Here, then, was one of the first and most important reasons why Joseph came to be hated and reviled by ministers and their congregations: the charge that all other faiths were offensive to God and their preachers corrupt. That accusation, they argued, was not simply wrong and insulting but damnable.

How dare a fourteen-year-old condemn centuries-old, established religions about which he knew nothing?

It stunned Joseph that the experience of "an obscure boy . . . of no consequence" would be dismissed so contemptuously by "men of high standing" and that they would later "create a bitter persecution" against him and unite to harm him. Still Joseph knew what he had seen, and he believed fervently that he had had a personal encounter with the Godhead, who said that none of the sects were worthy. But that fact left him isolated without a formal religion he could join and call his own.

No matter. He would continue as before. He worked on the farm and went treasure hunting in the hope of finding the wealth that would rescue him and his family from their crushing debts and periodic descents into grinding poverty. He wanted out of this kind of life—out of farming (he was not terribly good at it) and out of the anonymity of rural life. Not for him was the drudgery of farming. A quick-witted, ambitious boy, gifted with a soaring imagination, he soon demonstrated a talent for leadership and a personal need for attention and recognition. He was an outgoing and gregarious young man when playing or working with his friends. But at home in the quiet of his room or in the fields out of sight he was self-absorbed and intensely concerned about the salvation of his soul. His mother said he was much less inclined to read books than any of her other children. Like his father, he was "far more given to meditation and deep study."

He did have a wonderful sense of humor, however. At night he would regale his family with stories that "amused them" more than "could be imagined," claimed his mother. Other contemporaries repeatedly testified that he could be "joyously funny" when inspired. And he loved being the center of attention. What is more, his mother said, he would describe in colorful detail the "ancient inhabitants of this continent": the Indians, their dress, mode of travel, the animals they rode, their buildings and cities, their mode of warfare and religious worship—all of it conjured up through his lively imagination. He knew next to nothing about such things other than what was common folklore and what could be culled from the artifacts of Indian mounds in the area and other objects left behind by the tribes as they were pushed farther west. But what he did know he could describe with such vivid particulars and precision that his listeners believed he had a vast store of information on the subject. And because he had such a fertile imagination his telling of these "facts" was a performance in and of itself. One neighbor said that he could never relate a common occurrence in daily life without embellishing it with details that he spun from pure fantasy. As a result there was something compelling in what he said and the way he said it that riveted his listeners to his every word. And this despite a meager education. True, he could read, write, and do simple arithmetic, probably taught by his father, but that was about the sum total of his learning. Fortunately his mother's fierce intellect shone through him.

As the years passed Joseph grew to be a little over six feet tall, with sloping forehead, broad muscular shoulders and chest, blue eyes, aquiline nose, full lips, light brown hair, extended eyelashes, and bushy eyebrows. He had long legs, small hands, and large feet. His complexion was generally light, indeed pale. In brief, he was moderately handsome, with an ingratiating smile and "beautiful eyes," and he soon became "a great favorite with the ladies."

During this time he lived a relatively quiet life. The country suffered a severe financial depression in the Panic of 1819 that continued for several years. The Smiths struggled through it, but otherwise, as Lucy later said, nothing "occurred of very great importance." There were no further visions by anyone in the family. Even so, "different orders of religionists," the teenage Joseph wrote, continued to mock and ridicule him for what they called his alleged visitation by God, probably because he continued to tell people about it (which might indicate that he was trying to draw attention to himself) and to insist he was not lying.

It was at the height of this so-called harassment by both the "religious and irreligious," at a time when he did not know where to turn and had been "forbidden to join any of the religious sects," that Joseph said he suffered "all kinds of temptations . . . and frequently fell into many foolish errors, and displayed the weakness of youth, and the foibles of human nature . . . offensive in the sight of God." What sins were these? Sins of the flesh? After all he was a teenager and, like all his peers, he had to contend with raging hormones and the torment of puberty. But Joseph does not say what his temptations were, except to mention levity and an association with "jovial company." These may seem trivial to an average person and hardly mortal transgressions, but Joseph later insisted that they were out of character for someone who had been "called of God as I had been" and therefore were offensive to Him.

In the midst of this turmoil, on Sunday, September 21, 1823, at the age of seventeen, he went to bed and prayed that God would forgive all his "sins and follies" and make him worthy of salvation. He worked himself into an ecstatic state of longing and desire. Then suddenly, he reported, the room was enveloped by a light that was brighter than anything he had seen throughout his entire life. Brighter than noonday. And there by his bedside stood another "personage," suspended in the air. This vision wore a robe of "the most exquisite white-ness." His feet, arms, neck, and head were uncovered, as were his legs, a little above the ankles. The robe was open so that Joseph could see his chest. This vision was "glorified beyond description."

At first Joseph was frightened, he said, but the fear soon left him. The vision finally spoke, called the teenager by name, and said that he was a messenger from God and that his name was Moroni. Joseph just listened. Moroni said that God had "a work" for him to do, and because of it Joseph's name "should be both good and evil spoken of among all people."

He then told Joseph that there was a book, written on gold plates and hidden in a box, that gave an account of the "for-mer inhabitants of this continent." He also said that "the ful-ness of the everlasting Gospel was contained in it, as delivered by the Savior to the ancient inhabitants." Moreover, there were two stones set in the rim of "silver bows" which were fas-tened to a breastplate and constituted "what is called the Urim and Thummim" and were also deposited with the plates. These were seerstones that God had prepared for the purpose of translating the book. Moroni then warned Joseph against showing the Urim and Thummim or the plates to anyone else, except those who later would be designated to see them. If Joseph disobeyed, he would be "destroyed." Moroni then quoted from several passages in the Bible, particularly verses re-lated to the Second Coming of Christ and the end of the world, but some of them varied slightly from what Joseph knew of those texts.

As Moroni spoke the lad could see the place where the plates were deposited. The vision was so clear and distinct that when he later visited the spot he recognized it immediately.

With Moroni's final words quoting the Bible, the light in

the room began to fade, except for the light surrounding the messenger. Then a "conduit" opened up to heaven and Moroni ascended until he disappeared and the room was again dark.

Joseph lay in his bed, stupefied. He mulled over what had been said to him and what it all meant. As he meditated, the room became bright again and Moroni reappeared and repeated what he had previously said "without the least variation." Then the messenger told him of the "great judgments which were coming upon the earth, with great desolations by famine, sword and pestilence." These judgments, warned Moroni, would appear in the present generation. And with that frightening announcement, he again ascended into heaven.

Joseph could not sleep. He just lay in his bed "overwhelmed in astonishment." Moments later Moroni appeared for the third time to repeat all he had said before. But this time he cautioned the boy, "telling me that Satan would try to tempt me, in consequence of the indigent circumstances of my father's family, to get the plates for the purpose of getting rich," Joseph wrote. This Moroni forbade him to do. His sole object must be "to glorify God" and build His Kingdom. Otherwise he would never find the plates.

In the morning Joseph said nothing to the family but joined his father and his brother Alvin working in the field, reaping. All of a sudden Joseph stopped and seemed to be in a trance. "We must not slacken our hands," Alvin scolded him, "or we will not be able to complete our task."

Joseph began reaping again. Moments later he stopped. This time Joseph Sr. turned to his son and, noticing how pale he looked, directed him to return to the house and have his mother doctor him. The boy obeyed, but as he attempted to climb over a fence he fainted and lay there semiconscious. He was totally unaware of anything happening around him. Then he heard a voice calling him by name. He looked up and there stood Moroni once more above him surrounded by the same dazzling light he had seen before. The messenger repeated everything he had said the previous night, adding that the youth must go to his father and tell him of the vision and the commandments he had received.

Joseph came fully awake, roused himself, and returned to the field. In a torrent of words he blurted out all that had happened to him. And then something wonderful occurred. Instead of scolding the boy for shirking his work with a ridiculous story, his father listened intently and believed every word the lad spoke. The vision came from God, insisted Joseph Sr. You must "go and do as commanded by the messenger," he said, and find what had been promised.

The teenager went immediately to the hill where he knew the plates were buried, recognizing at once the place in his vision the night before. This was Hill Cumorah, of considerable size and the largest and most elevated in the area. It was in Manchester, Ontario County, New York, just a few miles from the Smith farm. On the west side of this hill, near the top, under a stone of enormous size, lay the plates. This stone was thick, with the center part visible above the ground but its edges covered with earth.

The first thing Joseph did when he reached the spot was remove the dirt surrounding the edges. Then, obtaining a lever, he pried the stone up to reveal a box formed by five stones set in "some kind of cement." Joseph looked into the box. He was stunned by what he saw. There lay the golden plates with strange markings on them, the seerstones, Urim and Thummim, and the breastplate. They rested on two stones laid crossways at the bottom of the box.

Joseph reached for these treasures but the messenger, who suddenly appeared, stopped him. The time for bringing them out and translating the plates, Moroni announced, had not yet arrived. Nor would it for another four years. He then directed the young man to come back precisely one year from that day and time, when he would meet him once again. Furthermore they were to continue to meet each year until the moment arrived for obtaining the plates. Accordingly, Joseph reported later, he returned to the spot as directed on September 22 of each succeeding year, and each time he found Moroni present. During these interviews he received further "instruction and intelligence" about what God was going to do and how and in what manner His Kingdom "was to be conducted in the final days."

Lucy claimed that Joseph could not have the plates until he had learned to keep the commandments of God. "Not only till he was willing," she declared, "but able to do it."

On the following evening when the family gathered together Joseph told them about the messenger and the plates. And during the next few days he kept up his claim to these mystical experiences. He said he continued to receive instructions from the Lord and explained to his family what he had been commanded to do. Entranced by this extraordinary tale, they hung on each word. Every day they worked harder to finish their chores before sunset. Lucy would prepare an early supper so "we will have a fine long evening" to listen to Joseph "tell us the great things which God has revealed" to him. But Joseph charged them all not to mention to another living soul what he related to them. It must be kept within the family circle, he warned, because "the world was so wicked that when they came to a knowledge of these things they would try to take our lives."

It delighted Lucy's soul to see her family all seated in a circle: father, mother, sons, and daughters, all giving "the most profound attention to a boy, eighteen years of age," as he described his supernatural experiences. It brought much happiness and tranquillity to the house, she said. It was "the sweetest union" possible.

And Joseph had found an audience to satisfy any need he might have had for attention. It was an audience that would grow with the years as he propounded God's plan of salvation and the redemption of the human family.

The happy scenes of Joseph conducting evening sessions on his visions ended with the tragic death of Alvin, the oldest child of the family. It seems that he came down with a severe stomach disorder and the doctor ordered a large dose of calomel, a compound of mercury and chlorine, which was a widely prescribed drug thought to have therapeutic properties. Instead it poisoned the unfortunate man. He died on November 19, 1823, at the age of twenty-five. Because Alvin was unchurched, it was presumed by some fastidious Christians that he had gone to hell. Later a rumor circulated that his body had been exhumed and dissected. Fearing its truth, the father dug up the remains and published a statement on September 30, 1824, in the *Wayne Sentinel* stating that he had found the body to be undisturbed.

A short time later a man by the name of Josiah Stowell (or Stoal) came to the Smith home to ask Joseph to assist him in digging for a silver mine. He had heard that the young man "possessed certain keys, by which he could discern things invisible to the natural eye." He wanted Joseph to help dig for the mine, said to be located on his property in Harmony, Pennsylvania, in the Susquehanna valley. Spaniards had allegedly worked it, and if Joseph would assist in the digging

Stowell was prepared to pay him fourteen dollars a month plus free board. Alvin's death had placed a greater burden on young Joseph to help support the family, which no doubt prompted him to accept this most unusual invitation.

In the fall of 1825 Joseph, his father, and several other diggers packed a few belongings and went on this treasure-hunting quest. At first young Smith had high expectations of finding an enormous treasure. It was later reported that the diggers fasted and prayed to break the charm protecting the treasure and that they even sprinkled the blood of a lamb on the chosen spot to propitiate the spirit below; but after a month of fruitless searching and digging the workers became discouraged and drifted away. The senior Smith also departed and returned home. But Joseph remained with Josiah Stowell and worked on his farm in South Bainbridge (now Afton), New York, just a short distance away. He also found other odd jobs and attended school in the winter.

It was during this period that Joseph had a serious brush with the law. In the spring of 1826 one of Stowell's nephews, Peter Bridgeman, swore out a warrant against him on the charge that he was a "disorderly person and an imposter," that he looked into a hat through a stone, "pretending to tell where a chest of dollars were buried." In his defense Joseph admitted that he had a seerstone, that he occasionally used it to find treasure, that he worked for Stowell and indeed had informed him of where he could find treasures, but that of late he had pretty much abandoned the practice of peering through stones because it hurt his eyes and made them sore. He insisted that he now declined any business having to do with crystal gazing. Other witnesses, including Stowell, testified, and it seems to be in doubt whether the justice of the peace found him guilty or not. It is unknown what, if any, sentence was passed, but the prosecution and trial were one of many that would dog Joseph for the remainder of his life. These lawsuits were apparently intended to harass him sufficiently to get him to shut up or run him out of town.

Evidently Joseph was quite sincere about giving up the world of divining rods and peepstones, although he did keep his special stone that he had dug up with his brother Alvin. But as for accepting invitations to hunt treasure, that was over and done with. He had matured, he said.

The cause of this change may have been the trial, but more likely it was the fact that at the age of twenty-one he had fallen in love with Emma Hale. Even though he had worked for Stowell, he and his father boarded at the home of Isaac Hale, a well-known hunter in the area, and it was here that he met Hale's dark-haired, shy, and winsome daughter Emma. On a brief trip home to keep his appointment with Moroni on September 22, he told his parents that he had been "very lonely" since Alvin's death and that he had decided to get married. If they had no objections he would marry Emma Hale, his "choice in preference to any other woman I have ever seen."

But Isaac Hale wanted no part of this money digger, this poor no-account "imposter," and he roared his refusal when Joseph asked for Emma's hand in marriage. To Isaac, Joseph was a "stranger, and followed a business that I could not approve."

Poor Emma. She undoubtedly loved this handsome "favorite" of the ladies, but she did not wish to offend her father and was surely concerned about their future and the kind of life she and Joseph would have together. The young man begged her to run away with him and live with his parents until they could get a home of their own. Lucy had made it clear she not only consented to the marriage but wanted the couple to live with them. At that point Josiah Stowell, who also approved of the marriage, invited Emma to his home. She later told her son that she had no intention of marrying when she visited Stowell. But during her visit Joseph appeared. She said she was "importuned" by both Joseph and Stowell, "and preferring to marry him to any other man I knew, I consented." The two were married in the house of Squire Zechariah Tarble in South Bainbridge on January 18, 1827. Joseph had turned twenty-one the month before, and Emma was twenty-two.

The couple moved back to Manchester and lived with his parents and the other Smith children for the next several months. During the summer Emma wrote her father and asked if she might claim the clothing and furniture that belonged to her. In reply her father assured her that they were hers for the taking, whereupon Joseph hired a neighbor, Peter Ingersoll, to help him and Emma transport the items back to Manchester.

When they arrived at Isaac Hale's home, the father soundly reprimanded Joseph. In a flood of tears he cried: "You have stolen my daughter and married her. I had much rather have followed her to her grave. You spend your time in digging for money—pretend to see in a stone, and thus try to deceive people."

Joseph also wept. He swore he had given up looking through stones. He could "not see in a stone now, nor never could; and that his former pretensions in that respect were all false." He then solemnly promised to give up crystal gazing and digging for treasure.

Hale responded that if he was serious and would move back to Pennsylvania and work for a living that he, Hale, would assist him in starting a business. Joseph accepted the offer and then he, Emma, and Ingersoll returned to Manchester.

Not much later Joseph went to the village on business but did not return at the expected hour. His family naturally became anxious. When he finally arrived his father queried him about the cause. Joseph simply dropped into a chair. He said nothing. The older man persisted. Finally, according to Lucy's account, Joseph smiled and said in a calm voice, "I have taken the severest chastisement that I have ever had in my life." His father stared at him and then angrily accused him of nosing into business that did not concern them.

"Stop, father, stop," young Joseph protested, "it was the angel of the Lord: as I passed by the hill of Cumorah, where the plates are, the angel met me, and said that I had not been engaged enough in the work of the Lord; that the time had come for the Record to be brought forth; and that I must be up and doing, and set myself about the things which God had commanded me to do. But, father, give yourself no uneasiness concerning the reprimand which I have received, for I know the course that I am to pursue, so all will be well."

"I know the course that I am to pursue." Clearly, the plates and the Urim and Thummim with the breastplate would have to be taken from their resting place. The four years had expired and it was time to unearth them. As instructed, he waited until September 22, 1827, and then returned to Hill Cumorah where he met Moroni, who turned the treasures over to him. But the angel charged him not to let them out of his care. If he did he would be "cut off." Joseph was responsible for them and must preserve them until Moroni called for their return.

Some critics have argued that Joseph concocted this story to avoid keeping his promise to his father-in-law. He had to figure out an escape from the dreary prospect of a life in business, so he claimed that he was finally given the golden plates and charged with translating them.

Be that as it may, Joseph dug up the treasure and about midnight entered his father's house and asked his mother if she had a chest with a lock and key. She said she knew instantly what it was for, but unfortunately she did not have what he wanted. "Never mind," he answered, "I can do very well for the present without it—be calm—all is right." With that Joseph and his wife left the house and did not return until morning.

Lucy was very anxious about what might happen. She was sure that by "some failure in keeping the commandments of God" all would be lost, but Joseph reassured her. "Do not be uneasy mother, all is right—see here, I have got a key." He handed her what looked like "two smooth three cornered diamonds set in glass, and the glasses were set in silver bows" that were connected to each other, she said, like "old fashioned spectacles." These were the seerstones, Urim and Thummin, and they really excited Joseph. He told a friend that with them he could see everything. "They are marvelous." He kept them constantly about his person and by the use of them he could tell in a moment whether the Record was in any danger. With them he hoped to translate the characters that were written on the plates and make what they said available to the world. Meanwhile he had his brother Hyrum find a chest with a good lock and key to keep the treasure; temporarily he concealed them in an old decayed birch log about three miles from the house, covering them over with the bark he had cut from the log.

Unfortunately the senior Smith had already told a "confidential friend" about the plates and word spread quickly and incited the envy of many in the community who began searching for "Joe Smith's gold bible." Fearing that these "devilish fools" would "thwart the purposes of the Almighty," Joseph gathered the plates from their hiding place, wrapped them in his linen smock, and started for home. Along the way he was attacked several times by would-be robbers but managed to escape. Once home he sent word to Hyrum to deliver the chest.

When it arrived he placed the plates inside and locked them up. But the seerstones, Urim and Thummim, he kept close to him.

After he rested a bit he walked into the kitchen where Josiah Stowell and a friend and neighbor, Joseph Knight, and several others were talking with his father and told them what had happened. Other neighbors gathered as well, for the news of the plates had circulated in the community and they wanted to hear more details. In fact, they asked to see these remarkable plates—even offering to pay for the privilege—but Joseph assured them that he could not do it, that the angel had forbade him from showing the Record to anyone.

A few townsfolk, especially those who had worked with Joseph in treasure hunting, felt that as former partners they had a right to these valuable plates. Joseph held them off as best he could, hiding the plates in different places in the succeeding weeks, but that did not stop these "wicked men." Using all manner of occult magic they searched everywhere to find them, without success.

However, Joseph did show the breastplate to his mother. It was, she later reported, wrapped in a thin muslin handkerchief, so thin, in fact, that she could see the glistening metal and recognize that it was concave on one side and convex on the other and extended downward from the neck to the approximate center of a man's stomach of extraordinary size. It had four straps with holes for fastening, of which two went over the shoulders and the other two were to be tied around the hips. She estimated that it was worth at least five hundred dollars.

Lucy never saw the golden plates. Joseph had been warned that any unauthorized person faced instant death to look upon them, just as had happened in the Old Testament when an unsanctioned individual inadvertently touched the Ark of the Covenant. He himself described them as about eight inches square and wafer thin. They were bound together with three huge rings and were engraved with what he said were "reformed Egyptian" characters.

Because of mounting pressure in Manchester to see and examine the plates, Joseph realized he could never translate them in peace and safety if he stayed in town. He would have to leave Palmyra to do it; but that created a problem. He was debt-ridden, and any sudden departure would bring his creditors chasing after him with subpoenas for his arrest. Fortunately the angel had revealed to Joseph that Martin Harris, a prosperous farmer, had been chosen to help in the translation of the plates. So Harris was summoned and informed of God's will. Harris was a religious seeker whose search for salvation had taken him from one Christian denomination to another. At different times he had been a Quaker, a Universalist, a Restorationist, a Baptist, and a Presbyterian. Since he had heard of "Joe Smith's golden bible" and wanted to hear more about it, he agreed without question to listen to what the young man had to say.

Joseph was very specific about his experiences, and very good at relating them, and what he said deeply impressed Harris. "If it is the devil's work," the farmer responded, "I will have nothing to do with it, but if it is the Lord's, you can have all the money necessary to bring it before the world." When the interview ended Harris returned home and prayed. He later said that God showed him that "it was his work, and that it was destined to bring in the fullness of his gospel to the gentiles." The Almighty revealed it "by the still small voice spoken in the soul."

Shortly thereafter Harris presented Joseph and his now pregnant wife with a gift of fifty dollars, which helped them pay off their debts. Once free of this burden, the couple packed their belongings in a wagon brought from Harmony by Emma's brother, Alva Hale, and headed for Pennsylvania.

Emma's father, Isaac Hale, was undoubtedly displeased that Joseph had not taken up his earlier offer to put him in business, but to assuage his annoyance and possibly win his approval he was told about the plates and even allowed to feel the weight of the chest in which they lay. However, he was not permitted to open the chest and inspect the contents. Outraged, he informed Joseph that "if there is any thing in my house . . . which I could not be allowed to look" at, then it must be taken away. Disappointed but obligated not to show the Record to any unauthorized person, the young man removed the chest from the house and hid it temporarily in the woods.

Subsequently, when the couple moved into a two-room house owned by Emma's brother, the chest was placed "in a box under our bed," and it lay there "for months," she later remembered. Sometimes there was no attempt at concealment and the plates sat on a table wrapped in a tablecloth. At one point Emma felt the plates, "tracing their outline and shape. They seemed to be pliable like thick paper," she said, "and would rustle with a metallic sound when the edges were moved by the thumb, as one does sometimes thumb the edges of the book."

Finally, in December 1827, Joseph began the task of translating the plates. The Record was about to be revealed.

Chapter 4

The Book of Mormon

TRANSLATING THE RECORD proved more complicated than originally supposed, since Joseph first had to study the strange-looking characters, which he called "reformed Egyptian," transcribe them, and then translate their meaning. To start he copied a "considerable number" of these characters from the plates and then translated a few of them by means of the Urim and Thummim. He worked steadily in Harmony, Pennsylvania, between December 1827 and February 1828, assisted by Emma, who wrote down what he dictated. She later said that her husband translated the first part using the Urim and Thummim but afterward he utilized a small, dark-colored stone. In his *History of the Church* Joseph simply stated that "through the medium of the Urim and Thummim I translated the record by the gift, and power of God."

When he began the translation he would dictate hour after hour. After returning from a meal or some other interruption, remembered Emma, "he would at once begin where he had left off, without either seeing the manuscript or having any portion of it read to him." No man could have done it, she declared, "unless he was inspired." She marveled at his achievement, considering how "unlearned and ignorant he was."

Joseph kept at the task for two months, both copying and translating. Then, in February, Martin Harris materialized, announcing that the Lord had appeared to him in a vision, showed him "the marvelous work he was about to do," and directed him to go to New York City and take with him some of the reformed Egyptian characters and translations, apparently to have them authenticated by a distinguished scholar of classical studies. Joseph consented to this mission and gave him several pages of text.

In New York Harris consulted Professor Charles Anthon of Columbia University, who was about as distinguished a classicist as anyone in America. Harris claimed that the professor gave him a certificate stating that the characters were true and the translation correct, "more so than any he had before seen translated from the Egyptian." Harris then showed him characters that had been copied but not yet translated, and Anthon identified them as Egyptian, Chaldaic, Assyrian, and Arabic and added that they were true characters. The professor then asked his visitor how he had obtained them. Harris explained that an angel of God had given them to a friend of his.

At that Anthon demanded the return of the certificate. He tore it up and told Harris that there was no such thing as "the ministering of angels." But he offered to translate the plates if they were brought to him. Harris said it was impossible because the plates were "sealed." "I cannot read a sealed book," the professor retorted.

However, in letters written in 1834 and 1841, Anthon told a much different story. He claimed that he was shown a mishmash of signs, symbols, and alphabets: Hebrew and Greek letters, stars, crosses, half moons, and other objects, ending in something that resembled the Mexican zodiac. In sum, he pronounced the whole a hoax to cheat poor Harris of his money. "The paper," he insisted, "contained any thing else but 'Egyptian Hieroglyphics.'"

Whatever the truth, Harris returned home after consulting another professor, a Dr. Samuel Latham Mitchell, who pronounced the characters true and the translation correct. Reassured by this endorsement, Harris was now convinced that Joseph had spoken and acted under the inspiration of God and that his work emanated from "divine impulses."

Harris's enthusiasm was such that he agreed to help with the translation. In a tiny attic room, starting in mid-April and continuing over the next two months, Joseph translated some 116 pages of foolscap paper, dictating his translation to Harris. Emma, in the meantime, gave birth to her firstborn, a son, Alvin, who died the day he was born, June 15, 1828.

Still denied the sight of the plates, Harris asked if he could take the 116 pages home to Palmyra to prove to his doubting wife, Dolly, that he was involved in a divine operation and not, as she suspected, a diabolical scheme concocted by a charlatan to cheat him out of his property. After repeated refusals, Joseph finally relented when the Lord granted him permission to allow Harris temporary possession of the writings on one condition—that he show them only to his wife; his wife's sister, Abigail Harris Cobb; his brother, Preserved; and his mother and father.

Once permission was granted and he had promised to abide by the condition, Harris hurried back home while Joseph remained behind to care for Emma, who had had a difficult delivery and was recovering from both the trauma of her ordeal and the loss of her child. But after a period of nearly three weeks with no communication from Harris, Joseph grew apprehensive over what might have happened to the manuscript. Concerned for his mental well-being, Emma urged him to return to Manchester, see Harris, and quiet his anxiety.

Leaving his wife in her mother's care, Joseph took the stage to Palmyra and walked the last twenty miles through a forest to his parents' home. Harris was summoned, but when he arrived his appearance startled everyone in the room. He dropped into a chair, put his hands to his temples, and cried out, "Oh, I have lost my soul! I have lost my soul!" Terrified, Joseph exclaimed, "Martin, have you lost that manuscript . . . and brought down condemnation upon my head, as well as your own?"

"Yes, it is gone," Martin sobbed, "and I know not where."

"Oh, my God!" Joseph exclaimed. "All is lost! all is lost! What shall I do?" He wept and groaned, clenching his hands and pacing the floor. "I well remember that day of darkness," his mother wrote, "both within and without. To us, at least, the heavens seemed clothed with blackness, and the earth shrouded with gloom."

Harris had put the manuscript in his wife's locked bureau for safekeeping. Then, in violation of the promise he had made, he revealed it to a friend. His wife was away when he attempted to show it to another neighbor and was forced to pick the lock, damaging the bureau in the process. His wife was outraged when she discovered what he had done and may have taken revenge by concealing the manuscript from her husband or destroying it. Whatever the truth, it had disappeared and Harris could not find it. Worse, he had revealed the existence of the "Golden Bible" to a number of friends. To this day it is not known what happened to the manuscript.

Heartsick, Joseph returned to his wife. He humbled himself "in mighty prayer before the Lord." He begged for mercy and forgiveness for having acted contrary to the divine will.

The angel appeared. He told Joseph that he had sinned in yielding the manuscript to a wicked man and as punishment the plates and the Urim and Thummim had been taken from him. They would be returned, the messenger said, "if you are very humble and penitent." If they were to be returned it would happen on September 22, the day of their annual meeting.

When the angel left him, Joseph continued praying and supplicating God "without cession," and on September 22, as the messenger had indicated, the seerstones and plates were returned to him. After a short respite in which he farmed and cared for his wife, he was finally instructed to resume his translation with Emma's help until such time as a suitable scribe sent by God would arrive to help him.

On April 5, 1829, the scribe arrived in the person of Oliver Cowdery. Twenty-two years old, unmarried, and a schoolteacher in Palmyra, he had come from Vermont, boarded with the Smiths, and quickly heard about the "Golden Bible" that Joseph had unearthed. Mesmerized by the story, he waited until the end of the school year and asked if he could accompany Samuel, one of the younger Smith children, who planned to visit Joseph. Samuel had just recovered from a long illness and intended to spend the spring with Joseph and Emma. Cowdery explained to the Smiths that their narrative of plates and revelations had been "working in my very bones. . . . I have made it a subject of prayer, and I firmly believe it is the will of the Lord that I should go. If there is a work for me to do in this thing, I am determined to attend to it."

And so Samuel and Oliver set out and reached Joseph's home after a long trip through wet and disagreeable weather. Joseph was immediately taken with the stranger and seemed to know that this was the scribe the Lord had promised. Something of a prophet himself in this age of countless prophets, Oliver brought with him a "rod of nature: said to contain spiritual qualities that could be used in divining."

Two days later Joseph recommenced the translation and it

moved along quite rapidly. Through revelations Joseph was forbidden to retranslate the first 116 missing pages, since the devil, he was told, would see to their publication in an altered form. The information contained in the lost manuscript would be included in the first part of *The Book of Mormon,* thus frustrating any satanic effort to distort the word of God. This story has been derided by some hostile non-Mormons as a clever feint by which Joseph protected himself in case the two versions were ever compared.

When Martin Harris had taken dictation, a blanket had hung between the two men to prevent the scribe from seeing the plates. Now Cowdery worked in the same room with Joseph but without the blanket. Instead the plates lay on the table covered with a cloth or sometimes uncovered altogether. Again Joseph would put the translators (as he called the seer-stones) into a hat, bury his face in it, draw it close around him to exclude all but "spiritual light," peer through the Urim and Thummim, read one character at a time, and then translate its meaning for Oliver to write down.

On May 15, 1829, in the midst of their labor, Joseph and Oliver went into the woods to pray and ask the Lord about baptism for the remission of sins, which had been mentioned in the translation of one of the plates. While they were lost in prayer, Joseph later reported, a messenger from heaven suddenly descended in a cloud of light. The messenger identified himself as John the Baptist and said that he acted under the direction of the Apostles Peter, James, and John, "who held the keys of the Priesthood of Melchizedek, which Priesthood, he said, would in due time be conferred on us." He further stated that Joseph should be called "the first Elder of the Church" to be established and Oliver the second. Then he laid hands on the two men and ordained them, saying: "*Upon you my fellow servants, in the name of Messiah, I confer the Priesthood of Aaron, which holds the keys of the ministering of angels, and of the gospel of repentance, and of baptism by immersion for the remission of sins; and this shall never be taken again from the earth until the sons of Levi do offer again an offering unto the Lord in righteousness.*"

This Hebraic priesthood of Aaron did not include the power of laying on of hands for the gift of the Holy Ghost but, said the messenger, that power (the priesthood of Melchizedek) would be conferred on them later. Go and be baptized, he commanded, whereupon they went to the Susquehanna River, where Joseph baptized Oliver, and Oliver baptized Joseph. After that Joseph laid his hands upon Oliver's head and ordained him to the Aaronic priesthood, and Oliver performed the same ritual on Joseph, just as the messenger had directed. Joseph claimed that he and Oliver were to keep secret "the circumstances of having received the Priesthood and our having been baptized, owing to a spirit of persecution which had already manifested itself in the neighborhood."

Several days later the Apostles Peter, James, and John, who held "the keys of the kingdom and of the Dispensation of the Fulness of Times" given them by the Savior, suddenly appeared to Joseph and Oliver and ordained them to the Melchizedek priesthood, thus empowering them to bestow the gifts of the Holy Ghost. The exact date for what Mormons call the restoration of the Melchizedek priesthood is unknown. But recent research by Mormon historians indicates that it probably took place between Colesville, New York, and Harmony around May 15 to 29, 1829. It occurred after Joseph and Oliver had traveled all night to escape their enemies—they had been preaching in Fayette, Manchester, and Colesville—and by morning they were so weary that they stopped to rest, where-upon the three apostles came to them and administered the or-dination. Thereafter all bearers of this priesthood were called "elders."

Because of what had become an ever-mounting "spirit of persecution" in the neighborhood among those who demanded to see "Joe Smith's Golden Bible" and who even threatened mob action if they were refused, Joseph and Oliver swore to keep secret what had happened to them. Any further mention of revelations or visitations was sure to stir greater excitement. Indeed, the danger had become so real that Emma's family, acting under "Divine providence," they claimed, used their in-fluence to help quiet the neighborhood and prevent possible violence. Having undergone a change of heart, they now felt that Joseph should be allowed to continue his work unim-peded, and they promised to protect him from unlawful ha-rassment.

About this time, according to Lucy Smith, her son received another command that he write to Oliver's friend David Whit-mer, who lived midway between Waterloo and Fayette in New York, asking him to come to Harmony immediately and trans-port Joseph and Oliver to his home to complete the translation of the plates. This was necessary because "an evil-designing people" were planning to take Joseph's life in order to prevent the work of God from being revealed to the world. Acting un-der divine inspiration, he said, Whitmer drove down to Penn-sylvania to pick up the two men. Meanwhile Joseph was instructed to surrender the plates to an angel for safekeeping. They would be returned to him on his arrival at the Whitmer home. When they reached the house the plates were duly re-turned, and the following day Joseph and Oliver resumed their translation, continuing without interruption until they completed their task, a total of sixty working days.*

Joseph immediately informed his parents that he had finished the translation and asked them to come to the Whitmer farm and bring Martin Harris with them. After they arrived, they all read the manuscript. "It would be superfluous for me to say," Lucy later wrote, ". . . that we rejoiced exceedingly."

In the translation several passages mentioned witnesses who would be permitted to see the plates so that the truth of their existence could be documented once and for all. Were the present company chosen to be the witnesses? Oliver, Martin, and David ardently queried Joseph, who in turn asked for a revelation.

The following morning, "after attending to the usual services, namely, reading, singing and praying," Joseph rose from his knees, approached Martin, and said, "Martin Harris, you have got to humble yourself before your God this day, that you may obtain a forgiveness of your sins. If you do, it is the will of God that you should look upon the plates, in company with Oliver Cowdery and David Whitmer."

Martin did in fact humble himself and a few minutes later he, Oliver, David, and Joseph walked into the woods and prayed, each taking turns, starting with Joseph.

Nothing happened. They tried again. Still nothing. At that, Martin rose, announced that he must be the cause of their fail-

*The Mormon historian Richard Bushman tells a slightly different story. According to his account, it was Oliver who wrote to David Whitmer because of financial necessity as well as the mounting danger from threatening townspeople. He further stated that the Whitmers knew Joseph and were keenly interested in the translation and most anxious to do all they could to help. Bushman, *Smith*, pp. 102–103.

ure, and took himself off to another part of the woods. The remaining three men, still kneeling, renewed their supplication, when suddenly a light appeared over their heads and an angel was revealed holding the plates. The messenger turned over the leaves one by one so that they could see them and the engravings distinctly visible on them.

The angel turned to David and said, "David, blessed is the Lord, and he that keeps his commandments." Then a voice, called out from the light, "These plates have been revealed by the power of God, and they have been translated by the power of God. The translation of them which you have seen is correct, and I command you to bear record of what you now see and hear."

After the angel departed, Joseph raced after Martin and begged him to pray with him. At length the same vision as before appeared and revealed the plates. Martin cried out "in an ecstasy of joy." He rose to his feet and shouted, "'Tis enough; 'tis enough; mine eyes have beheld; mine eyes have beheld." Then, like any attendant at a camp meeting during the Great Awakening, he raised his voice to proclaim God's mercy and goodness. "Hosanna! Hosanna!" he shouted. Blessed be the Lord.

The four men returned to the house in a state of exultation.

Mormons have no difficulty accepting this event with the utmost faith in its veracity. Non-Mormons who are skeptical of any divine appearance credit the occurrence either to Joseph's extraordinary talent at mesmerizing those around him and making them believe the apparition he described, or to the fact that they were all products of the Second Great Awakening and after praying on their knees for hours were caught up in a religious frenzy and were conditioned to believe that they saw an angel and the plates. And some have suggested they were part of a conspiracy for whatever personal gain—perhaps sharing in the profits from the sale of the published book—to palm Joseph off as a prophet. In sum, all wittingly participated in a colossal fraud.

However one wishes to interpret the event, David, Oliver, and Martin signed a statement that gave testimony to what they had seen:

> Be it known unto all nations, kindreds, tongues and people . . . that we, through the grace of God . . . have seen the plates that contain this record. . . . And we also know that they have been translated by the gift and power of God . . . ; wherefore we know of a surety that the work as true. And we also testify that we have seen the engravings which are upon the plates; and they have been shown unto us by the power of God, and not of man. And we declare . . . that an angel of God came down from heaven . . . and he brought and laid before our eyes . . . the plates and the engravings thereon.

The document was signed by Oliver Cowdery, David Whitmer, and Martin Harris. All three men later quarreled with Joseph and left the Church, but, as Mormons are quick to point out, none of them ever repudiated their statement.

Several days later Joseph Sr., his sons Hyrum and Samuel, and the four Whitmer sons—Christian, Jacob, Peter Jr., and John—together with their brother-in-law Hiram Page, went to a grove where the family usually prayed and offered up "their secret devotions to God." There, acting in accordance with a revelation he said he had received, Joseph showed them the plates. All eight later signed a statement attesting that "Joseph Smith, Jun. . . . has shown unto us the plates of which hath been spoken" and that these plates all had the appearance of gold. They concluded their statement with the words "And we lie not, God bearing witness of it."

The difference between the testimony of the three original witnesses and that of the eight is the manner in which the plates were revealed. The three experienced "the glory and power of God and the ministration of an angel." For the eight, it was a simple presentation by Joseph.

After the eight had seen the plates and returned to the house, the angel appeared once again to Joseph and received the plates from his hands. But some skeptics prefer to believe that this return of the plates to the angel was a convenient way for Joseph to fend off any future demands for evidence of their existence.

Joseph was now determined to publish his translation. He obtained a copyright on June 11, 1829, from the clerk of the Northern District of New York and persuaded Egbert B. Grandin, a printer, bookseller, and editor and publisher of the local newspaper the *Wayne Sentinel,* to print five thousand copies. Martin Harris mortgaged his farm for three thousand dollars as security; in 1831 he sold the farm to satisfy the obligation.

The Book of Mormon: Another Testament of Jesus Christ, published on March 26, 1830, and sold initially for $1.25, is regarded by Mormons as a part of holy scripture. It claims to recount God's interaction with the native inhabitants of the American continent. Like the Old Testament, it comprises a series of books written by a number of prophets. They were transcribed on golden plates, the words of which were quoted and abridged by a prophet-historian named Mormon who died around A.D. 385. After Mormon completed his writings, he delivered the plates to his son Moroni, who added material of his own and then hid them in the Hill Cumorah where Joseph Smith discovered them on September 22, 1823.

The work starts with the book of the Hebrew prophet Nephi, who left Jerusalem around 600 B.C. and journeyed to America with his father, Lehi, also a prophet. Nephi had three older brothers—Laman, Lemuel, and Sam—and two younger brothers, Jacob and Joseph. On his father's death, Nephi won the allegiance of Sam, Jacob, and Joseph. The two older brothers were jealous, and in the conflict that followed the family split apart, with Nephi and his followers migrating to another part of the continent. The Nephites were peace-loving and kept God's commandments. The followers of Laman and Lemuel, however, were cursed by the Lord because of their wickedness and He "did cause a skin of blackness to come upon them." These are the Lamanites. They had been white but the color of their skin was changed "that they might not be enticing unto my people," the Nephites, who "were white and exceeding fair and delightful."

Thus, two separate tribes developed in America, and it is assumed today by Mormons that present-day Native Americans are the descendants of the Lamanites, who originated in Israel.

Then, following His crucifixion and resurrection from the dead in Jerusalem, Jesus appeared among the Nephites in America and preached His message of love and redemption. For the next two hundred years, the two tribes lived together in peace. Unfortunately Satan worked his wiles on the population and the tribes resorted to war once again. As the Lamanites and Nephites prepared for one final battle, Mormon knew he must preserve the writings of the previous prophets. He compiled what is now known as *The Book of Mormon*, using "reformed Egyptian" as it had been handed down to him.* In the ensuing battle the Lamanites slaughtered the Nephites, and Mormon was mortally wounded. He turned the plates over to Moroni, who lived another thirty-six years and abridged twenty-four additional plates, called the Book of Ether, which had been found and translated several hundred years earlier. Moroni included only a portion of these plates, omitting the section of the account from the creation of the world to the building of the Tower of Babel.

The people described in the Book of Ether were called Jaredites, after their first leader, Jared. They migrated to America around 2500 B.C., well before the arrival of the Nephites and Lamanites, coming "directly from the Tower of Babel" and sailing in eight watertight barges. There were "wars, dissensions, and wickedness" described in these plates, and Ether witnessed the final destruction of the Jaredites. But Ether tells of a New Jerusalem to be built in America upon "the remnant of the seed of Joseph," an obvious reference to Joseph Smith.

After Moroni had completed the abridgment of the Book of Ether, he wrote his own book, adding comments about the practices of the Church as established during Christ's ministry, along with three epistles from Mormon. He then closed the record by appealing to all who should read *The Book of Mormon* to "come unto Christ, and be perfected in him, and deny yourselves of all ungodliness." He bade them farewell until such time as he would meet them "before the pleasing bar of the

---

*In writing his account Mormon said he used "reformed Egyptian" as it had been handed down to him. Had the plates been large enough, he added, he would have written in Hebrew, and had he done so there would not have been any "imperfection in our record."

great Jehovah, the Eternal Judge of both the quick and the dead. Amen."

The Book of Mormon is an extraordinary work in several particulars. It was "translated" in record time by an uneducated but highly imaginative zealot steeped in the religious fervor of his age. The work is a religious narrative of political and military history, shot through with intrigue, prophecy, admonitions, sermons, conversions, religious conflicts, and profound theological conundrums that have engaged men's minds over centuries. It is a complex work, running well over six hundred pages and involving several hundred individually named participants.

Of the fifteen books that make up *The Book of Mormon,** the first six are claimed to have been written by their original authors and remain untouched by later editors. These include the two books of Nephi and the books of Jacob, Enos, Jarom, and Omni. At that point Mormon took over the narrative, working from materials available to him and interjecting quotations from other prophets, including Nephi, so that two and sometimes three voices are present in whatever is being narrated or discussed.

The *Book* as translated by Joseph borrows heavily from the King James Bible in both concepts and language. It even sounds biblical, with repeated expressions like "and it came to pass," "verily I say unto you," "for behold," "and whosoever," and so on. In his translation, Joseph had a firm grasp of the

---

*These fifteen books are: First Book of Nephi; Second Book of Nephi; Book of Jacob; Book of Enos; Book of Jarom; Book of Omni; The Words of Mormon; Book of Mosiah; Book of Alma; Book of Helaman; Third Nephi; Fourth Nephi; Book of Mormon; Book of Ether; Book of Moroni.

style, rhythm, and sounds of the Bible, and he used them to striking effect.

But the *Book* is also an American work of the early nineteenth century. It has a distinctly American character. It is a story about people who crossed an ocean and settled in a wilderness. It is a story of bringing the Gospel to the Americas. It is a story that people of the Jacksonian era could easily relate to and understand because it is part of a very American tradition. Moreover, it radiates revivalist passion, frontier culture and folklore, popular concepts about Indians, and the democratic impulses and political movements of its time. And it continues to speak to people today around the world.

A small example of its American character is its concern with secret societies, reflecting somewhat the series of violent demonstrations over Freemasonry during the Jacksonian era. This outburst resulted in 1826 from the disappearance and murder of a Mason by the name of William Morgan living in Batavia, New York, who became involved in a dispute with his lodge brothers and wrote a book disclosing Masonic secrets. When warnings failed to dissuade him from publishing his work, he was arrested for indebtedness. After his bail was paid he was seized as he left jail and probably taken to the Niagara River and drowned. His mysterious disappearance and the discovery of a disfigured corpse on the shore of Lake Ontario engulfed western New York in wild excitement. Masons were denounced for their membership in an organization committed to kidnapping and murder to protect their secret signs, handshakes, passwords, and other mysteries. They were accused of many unsolved crimes, and their rituals condemned as demonic. Because Masons were believed to be entrenched in business, the courts, and politics itself, an Anti-Masonic party sprang up and spread throughout New York and neighboring states. It was the first third party in American history and the first party to hold a national convention to nominate candidates for president and vice president.

Joseph Smith was translating *The Book of Mormon* at the height of this political upheaval. Not surprisingly there are passages in the *Book* about the Gadiantons, who took oaths to conceal their crimes and identified each other with "secret signs" and "secret words." And "they did enter into a covenant one with another . . . administered by the devil, to combine against all righteousness." Ironically, Joseph himself later joined the Masonic order.

Another example of the contemporaneousness of *The Book of Mormon* is the recognition and importance of seerstones. The Book of Ether claims that seerstones were placed in the vessels that transported the Jaredites to America. "And thus the Lord caused stones to shine in darkness, to give light unto men, women, and children, that they might not cross the great waters in darkness."

Naturally enough *The Book of Mormon* addresses all the great religious questions and controversies that raged within the Burned-Over District. According to a leading contemporary critic, Alexander Campbell, these topics include the Trinity, the fall of man, justification, redemption, repentance, transubstantiation, the call to the ministry, religious experience, the question of who may baptize, fasting, the general resurrection, and eternal punishment. And there is nothing ambiguous in the book's pronouncements. They are stern and absolute. No doubt virtually all of Joseph's experiences as a young man growing up in western New York, digging for treasure, and farming can be found in the book, including variations on his father's dreams or visions. This colossal work represents Joseph's thinking on whatever passed before his conscious and subconscious mind.

As for its literary worth, it must be admitted that long stretches of *The Book of Mormon* are deadly dull, despite all the mayhem, wars, and human carnage spread throughout. More times than not, a sentence begins with the word *and*. It has also been estimated that the phrase "and it came to pass" is repeated two thousand times. Mark Twain called the work "chloroform in print."

The publication of the book brought Joseph Smith immediate notoriety. After all, this was the very stuff to excite the interest of religious people—and skeptics too. Newspapers around the state and in Vermont and Ohio took notice of it, frequently with scathing criticism. The *Rochester Daily Advertiser,* for example, called the book blasphemous, superstitious, and a fraud upon all right-thinking Christians. The *Palmyra Freeman* labeled it "the greatest piece of superstition that has come to our knowledge." Within a year Joseph Smith Jr. and his book even caught the attention of the renowned editor James Gordon Bennett, who wrote in the *New York Courier and Enquirer:* "You have heard of MORMONISM—who has not? Paragraph has followed paragraph in the newspapers recounting the movements, detailing their opinions and surprising distant readers with the traits of a singularly new religious sect."

Perhaps only a few at first would read *The Book of Mormon*—initial sales were quite slow—but many of those who did read it were powerfully and lastingly affected by it. It changed their lives and the course of religious history in the United States.

Chapter 5

Organizing the Church
of Christ

AT THE TIME Joseph published *The Book of Mormon,* Andrew Jackson had been elected the seventh president of the United States, much to the consternation of those who feared he might prove to be another Napoleon and set up a dictatorship. After all, he had few qualifications for the high office he had won, other than his military exploits. But those exploits excited the admiration and gratitude of most Americans, who believed he would bring strong leadership to the office. It was the beginning of the long love affair Americans would have with their victorious generals.

Jackson's overwhelming election over John Quincy Adams occurred in 1828 after a singularly bitter and filthy campaign by both parties, indicating that something quite profound had occurred in American politics. New western and southern states had been admitted to the Union without any property or religious qualification for voting or holding office, and eastern states followed in the 1820s by adopting universal white manhood suffrage. Quite obviously the nation was headed in a new direction politically. The Republic, founded only a few short decades earlier, was evolving into a democracy, although many more decades passed before African-Americans, women, and Native Americans were granted voting rights. But many recognized at the time that this 1828 election, with its parades, barbecues, party insignias, slogans, songs, and gutter tactics, had inaugurated a new era in political history. As one woman in Salisbury, North Carolina, exclaimed on hearing of Jackson's nomination, "What! Jackson up for the President? *Jackson? Andrew* Jackson? The Jackson who used to live in Salisbury? . . . Well if Andrew Jackson can be President, anybody can!"

Americans soon discovered their new president was a thoroughgoing democrat. To be sure, he was a tough and determined leader who vigorously exercised all his presidential powers. Still he believed passionately in the people. "The people are the government," he repeatedly argued, "the sovereign power." In his inaugural address before twenty thousand people jammed around the Capitol building, he insisted that "the majority is to govern." He frankly believed and stated that in government there must be "no distinction between the rich and poor, the great and ignoble."

And Andrew Jackson's eight years in office reflected those beliefs. He instituted a system of rotation for government office which his enemies called a "spoils system." He destroyed the Second National Bank with a veto because he believed that it used its wealth and power to control elections and dictate congressional legislation. "Every man is equally entitled to protection by law," he wrote in the veto message; "but when the laws . . . grant titles, gratuities, and exclusive privileges, to make the rich richer and the potent more powerful, the humble members of society—the farmers, mechanics, and laborers— . . . have a right to complain of the injustice of their Government." He also insisted that Native Americans be moved west of the Mississippi River where they would cease to endanger national security. Had the British invasion and the uprising of the Creek Indians in the Creek War of 1813–1814 been synchronized, he declared, the outcome of the battle of New Orleans might have been far different and much more devastating for the United States.

Like their government and their new leaders, the American people were also changing in significant ways. Men and women who had once been colonists with a European culture were now distinctly American in their dress, speech, and behavior. George Washington in powdered wig, silk stockings, low-heel pumps, and shirts with ruffled collar and cuffs looked far different from Andrew Jackson in his plain shirt, tie, and trousers. Foreign visitors like Alexis de Tocqueville came to inspect this new vibrant country and its people. His classic work *Democracy in America* sharply identified many of the essential elements of American life and government. "The people reign in the American political world," he wrote, "as the Deity does in the universe. They are the cause and aim of all things; everything comes from them, and everything is absorbed in them."

"Go ahead," another visitor said, was a phrase that seemed to define this nation. It was "the real motto of the country." In fact "the whole continent presents a scene of *scrambling* and roars with greedy hurry." The age, agreed Senator Daniel Webster of Massachusetts, "is full of excitement" and rapid change.

Ironically, in the midst of this Second Great Awakening, Americans were building a materialistic society, one dedicated to business, trade, and the acquisition of wealth. They were committed, said Tocqueville, to the belief "that man is endowed with an indefinite faculty for improvement" and to "the indefinite perfectibility of man." In practical terms the "perfectibility of man" meant, of course, social reform.

Americans saw the evils in their society brought about by the Industrial Revolution, the market revolution, and the transportation revolution and felt they could eradicate them through concerted action. So they organized themselves, held meetings, collected money, and issued printed propaganda to advance such causes as abolition, women's rights, temperance, penal and mental health reform, education and labor reform, and many others. "The demon of reform" had been loosed upon the country, declared Ralph Waldo Emerson, and an army of volunteers, including people like Susan B. Anthony, Elizabeth Cady Stanton, Orestes Brownson, Dorothea L. Dix, Neal Dow, William Lloyd Garrison, Horace Mann, and thousands of others, joined together to scourge the nation of the social blight that disfigured it.

As might be expected, the churches provided many of these volunteers. "The evils have been exhibited," preached Charles Grandison Finney, the great revivalist, and Christians cannot "remain neutral and keep still" and expect to "enjoy the approbation and blessing of God." They must be active. They must extirpate these evils.

In a different way Joseph Smith Jr. became very active in extirpating evil once he completed the translation of *The Book of Mormon*. Even before it was published he had begun to attract a number of followers and think about organizing a church to "restore" Christianity. It would appear that around June 1829 he began to preach this new religion, and he found the people of Seneca County very receptive. "Many opened their houses to us," he later wrote, "in order that we might have an opportunity of meeting with our friends for the purpose of instruction and explanation." Joseph turned out to be an excellent preacher, once the "spirit" stirred within him, and the curious listened in fascination and awe to his incredible accounts of his mystical life and the truths that had been revealed to him. Slowly, as word of the new religion began to circulate in nearby communities, the number of believers increased.

The next step was obvious. In order to spread this restored

Gospel of Christ he needed to establish a church, just as any number of men and women during the Second Great Awakening had done. Mother Ann Lee had organized the Shakers; Alexander Campbell founded the Disciples of Christ and began the era's "Restoration Movement" to renew the purity of early Christianity; and William Miller started a crusade that evolved into the Seventh Day Adventists.

In a new revelation Joseph Smith declared that he had been instructed to found the Church of Christ, as it was initially called. In the spring of 1830, when *The Book of Mormon* was still in the hands of the printer, he informed his friend and benefactor Joseph Knight that God had decreed that "there must be a church formed." To that end a meeting was held in David Whitmer's farmhouse on Tuesday, April 6, 1830, in the town of Fayette, Seneca County, New York. Between thirty-five and fifty-five people gathered, and of that number six men formally "organized" the Church. These six consisted of Joseph, his brothers Hyrum and Samuel, Oliver Cowdery, and Peter and David Whitmer. The meeting began with prayer. Then Joseph asked whether all those present were willing to accept the six as their teachers in "the things of the Kingdom of God, and whether they were satisfied that we should proceed and be organized as a church." The group unanimously consented, whereupon Joseph laid his hands upon Oliver and ordained him "as Elder of the Church of Jesus Christ of Latter-day Saints," after which Oliver ordained Joseph. The group then blessed bread and ate it and blessed wine and drank it. Following this ritual Joseph and Oliver laid hands on each individual member present "that they might receive the gift of the Holy Ghost and be confirmed members of the church of Christ." Joseph later wrote that during the celebration the Holy Ghost descended upon them and suddenly some of the men began prophesying; but all praised the Lord "and rejoiced exceedingly."

While in this euphoric state Joseph received a command from the Lord to ordain others "to different offices of the Priesthood, according as the Spirit manifested unto us." He began by selecting those offices mentioned in *The Book of Mormon,* especially those in the Nephite churches. These included elders, priests, and teachers. Joseph and Oliver were elders who had been designated apostles sometime in late May 1829 when they had received the priesthood of Melchizedek; the elders would be part of a larger group called the Quorum of Twelve Apostles, similar to those in the New Testament, who would govern the Church and go into the world and preach this restored Gospel of Jesus Christ. Elders were empowered to distribute bread and wine in commemoration of Christ's passion and death, baptize, and invoke the Holy Ghost through the laying on of hands. As such they held the highest rank in the organization. Priests exercised all the power of the elders, except that they could not bestow the gifts of the Holy Ghost, ordain elders, or bless children. They could ordain other priests, teachers, and deacons but only on the authority of the elders. Teachers and deacons acted as assistants to the priests but had no specific function other than watching over the well-being of Church members.

At meetings the elders presided. In their absence priests or teachers could conduct services. Although it was not formally enunciated, it soon became the practice to ordain every worthy male member. But of paramount significance was the revelation on the day of the Church's organization concerning Joseph himself. "Behold there shall be a record kept among you; and in it thou shalt be called a seer, a translator, a prophet, an apostle of Jesus Christ, an elder of the church through the will of God the Father, and the grace of your Lord Jesus Christ." Henceforth members of the Church were to heed the words and commandments which Joseph would give them as coming directly from the Lord God and behold, "the gates of hell shall not prevail against you."

Hereafter Mormons came to refer to Joseph as "the Prophet." He was the first seer, translator, and prophet. Each leader of the Church who followed him had the titles prophet, seer, and revelator. The meanings of translator and prophet are clear enough, but the term *seer* needs explanation. According to the Book of Mosiah in *The Book of Mormon,* a seer is greater than a prophet in that "a seer can know of things which are past" as well as "hidden things" and "secret things."

Thus the organization of the Church was autocratic in the distribution of authority, but since every worthy male was ordained into the priesthood it rested on a democratic base just like political organizations during the Jacksonian era. And this induced a comradeship and a sense of oneness with the Church, thereby providing it with enormous internal strength. Virtually every man had a title, be it deacon, teacher, priest, elder, or one of the other offices that came later, and these involved duties and responsibilities. The Church as organized, therefore, was and is rigidly paternalistic—another reason for its appeal to men during an age in which profound changes were taking place between men and women and within the family.

This "gender revolution" was particularly important. As the Industrial Revolution developed after the War of 1812, it shifted income-producing labor from the home to the factory; it also caused agriculture to become more commercialized. As a result, the role of women became less that of partners in working small farms and more caretakers in the home. While men worked in factories or private business or farmed ever-larger stretches of land, women tended to engage exclusively in domestic tasks, such as cooking, sewing, and housekeeping. The role of women changed dramatically in society and, except for teaching and nursing, they were considered unfit for business or the professions. They were "reduced" to simply running the household and rearing children. They necessarily became the moral guardians of the home and were expected to provide religious instruction to the children in the family and serve as an example of the highest ethical and moral standards in society. The Jacksonian age placed a greater value and respect on the singular virtues of a woman and on her role as wife and mother. Women, and mothers in particular, were placed on a pedestal for all to admire and honor. But God help a woman if she fell off it. This "cult of domesticity," as it has been called, drastically redefined gender relationships.

This cult was especially strong among Mormons and remains so today. From the beginning Mormon women played a very limited role in the operation of the Church. They were subservient to men and were expected to provide proper homes that reflected Mormon belief and values.

Several men who attended the first organizational meeting came forward to be received into the Church, including Joseph Smith Sr. and Martin Harris. They were baptized by immersion. When his father rose out of the water after his baptism his son cried out "with tears of joy. 'Oh, my God! have I lived to see my own father baptised into the true Church of Jesus Christ!'" Lucy was also baptized, to Joseph's "great joy and consolation," as were her daughters. Shortly thereafter all the Smith sons were ordained as priests, even Don Carlos, who was fourteen. Today, worthy young men are ordained to the priesthood at the age of twelve.

Five days later, on Sunday, April 11, 1830, Oliver Cowdery inaugurated the public ministry of the Church of Christ when he preached at a meeting in Peter Whitmer's house in Fayette. A large number of people attended because "marvelous things" were said to have happened among believing Mormons and a great many "seekers" wanted to hear this new Gospel and perhaps share in the redemptive powers it offered.

At about this time it was reported that Joseph visited his benefactor Joseph Knight and had a long conversation with Knight's son Newel, who suffered "very much in mind." In addition Newel's body behaved "in a very strange manner. His visage and limbs distorted and twisted in every shape and appearance possible to imagine." He was even physically raised up and tossed around the room of his apartment "most fearfully." Scared half out of his wits, the poor man claimed that the devil was inside him and begged Joseph to "cast him out." Joseph responded, "If you know that I can, it shall be done," whereupon he "rebuked the devil" and commanded in the name of Jesus Christ that he depart. Immediately the devil was cast out, or so it was reported, and Newel's contortions ceased. His appearance resumed its natural color and "the Spirit of the Lord descended upon him." Joseph declared this exorcism the first miracle of the Church.

As the reputation of Mormonism spread, the first "conference" as an organized Church was held on June 9, 1830, in Fayette, following a revelation to Joseph in April that "the several elders composing this church of Christ are to meet in conference." Thirty members assembled along with a number of other believers and "those anxious to learn." The congregation began with prayers and hymns, followed by the distribution of "the emblems of the body and blood of our Lord Jesus Christ." They then ordained individual members to the various offices of the priesthood. This was the beginning of what became—and still is—a regular semiannual general conference, at which time Church officers are "sustained" by conference vote, usually unanimously. At these conferences, officials and converts also receive certificates of ordination or membership, and all present hear the announcement of new revelations.

One revelation of singular importance, a doctrine that is fundamental to the Mormon faith, is the belief that the authority of the Church of Christ had been lost because of corruption from the second century A.D. to the 1820s, when the true Church was restored by a latter-day revelation to Joseph Smith Jr. That is why followers of the Prophet call themselves "Latter-day Saints." This sense of restoration of what was lost gives Mormonism one of its distinctive attributes among Christian faiths.

In a separate revelation concerning the organization and selection of apostles who would later serve as a Quorum of Twelve Apostles, Joseph had been reminded that these apostles must "go into all the world to preach my gospel unto every creature." Therefore, on June 13, he sent his brother Samuel on a mission to Livonia, a short distance southwest of Palmyra, to preach and, if possible, sell *The Book of Mormon*.

So Samuel sallied forth, and along the way he stopped at a number of places to try to interest listeners in his Church and the book he had to sell. Quite regularly he was summarily "turned out of doors as soon as he declared his principles." But at one stop he did better. A poor widow woman listened intently as he outlined the history contained in *The Book of Mormon* and she "believed all that he told her." She had no money to buy the book, whereupon Samuel gave her a copy. He presented another copy to a family in upstate New York, and one of the family members, Brigham Young, picked it up and read it. "[I] sought to become acquainted with the people who professed to believe it," he declared. And suddenly he too believed it. When Young later met Joseph, the two men were irresistibly drawn to each other by the unusual qualities of their personalities: Young with his uncommon intelligence and overwhelming zest and enthusiasm, Joseph with his tremendous creative energy and verbal fluency.

Thus began the intense missionary work of the Church and the practice of presenting a free copy of *The Book of Mormon* to all who show genuine interest.

The initial and ultimate success of Mormonism was in no small part the result of its organized missionary activity and zeal. Like so many secular reform groups of this era, the Mormon Church propagated its faith in nearby towns and communities, and then slowly and steadily reached farther out. The first year at least sixteen missionaries were dispatched, including Joseph Sr. and his fourteen-year-old son Don Carlos, and the following year some fifty-eight missionaries fanned out to spread the word. This proselytizing became an art and today has been developed into a science in which thousands of Mormons circle the globe. At first young men took on the responsibility of spreading Joseph's message. Today they—and women too—frequently interrupt their college careers or professional work for up to two years to disseminate the gospel of Mormonism. They are expertly trained and have become excellent proselytizers for their faith. Joseph intuitively knew how important this work would be in expanding his Church, and the early missionaries he sent out attracted dozens and later hundreds and thousands of converts by their ardor and enthusiasm. As the number of these missionaries increased, they headed in every direction and over the next several years penetrated New England and Canada and even traveled west to the frontier. Many of them paid particular attention to Indians, whom they considered to be descendants of the Israelites, especially those across the Mississippi River.

Joseph demonstrated remarkable administrative skills in establishing the Church, shaping its focus and guiding its future direction. He appointed the leaders and those charged with organizing the people under the hierarchical structure he created. Indeed the unique leadership of the Church in its formative years explains in large measure its early success, first with Joseph Smith and, upon his death, with Brigham Young. These two men guided the Church to its full organizational growth.

Besides the proselytizing skills of its members, other reasons explain the immediate and phenomenal success that the Mormon Church achieved. First, there are no clergymen in the Mormon Church, a fact that appealed to many Americans who abominated privilege and deference in this democratic age. All worthy males are ordained in the Church and become an integral part of its operation, not simply passive statistics of a vast congregation who leave matters in the hands of a few. Each male has a function, duty, and responsibility. At a time when universal white manhood suffrage had been attained and when women had been "relegated to a pedestal position," this feature of the Church proved especially attractive.

Another reason for Mormon success was that a distinct change had occurred in the country with regard to religion and those who preached and directed it. No longer were university-trained clerics revered as they had been in the past. People wanted preachers who could rouse their emotions and offer them dramatic evidence of their faith and commitment. Joseph Smith Jr. fitted this mold to perfection. His was a new voice, a dramatic voice, a certain voice, a voice that throbbed with conviction and seemed to many to be divinely inspired. He claimed direct and frequent communication with God—and the people believed him. He offered to ordinary citizens, especially the poor, a sense of self-worth and belonging. In a constantly changing world, one in which the future seemed so uncertain, his followers found an identity in a community of other believers. They found meaning and direction in their lives. The Mormon Church met some of their deepest psychological and emotional needs because to them it offered a guarantee of truth.

Joseph himself was a man of compelling charisma, charm, and persuasiveness, a man absolutely convinced that his religious authority came directly from God. "I have felt to rejoice exceedingly," said one convert, "in what I saw of brother Joseph, for in his public and private career he carried with him the Spirit of the Almighty, and he manifested a greatness of soul which I had never seen in any other man." And when he preached, reported another member of the congregation, he would get caught up in what he had experienced and the authority he possessed and his voice became "very strong and powerful and seemed to affect the whole audience with the feeling that he was honest and sincere. It certainly influenced me in this way and made impressions upon me that remain until the present day."

Most important, Joseph provided a new kind of revelation, a new work of scripture, a new bible. He gave his followers *The Book of Mormon,* a written commitment of divine love and salvation, and that book imbued believers with a sense that their faith had a power no other sect possessed: divine authority. "All old covenants," said the Lord in a revelation to Joseph in

April 1830, "have I caused to be done away in this thing; and this is a new and an everlasting covenant, even that which was from the beginning."

One of the most powerful factors operating within Mormonism that explains much of its success is the sense of collective responsibility for the welfare of all its members. Almost from the beginning Mormons took care of their own. The poor among them—and there were many impoverished converts—found an unstinting hand ready to feed, clothe, and help them get settled within the community. They found hope and comradeship. Not surprisingly, therefore, many of the most desperate in society were attracted to this new religion. And this attribute of sharing and providing for the least of its members makes the Church especially distinctive today.

Finally, one of the most attractive aspects of the Mormon Church at this time was that it was rooted deeply in the American experience. It can rightly be called "an American religion." Despite its roots in the Middle East, it originated, grew, and blossomed in the United States. It explained the origin of Native Americans; it located the Garden of Eden in Jackson County, Missouri; and it revealed that Jesus returned to America after His resurrection and that the Second Coming would occur in the United States.

Joseph's teachings about Mormon, Moroni, golden plates, and the rest proved a burden for some because they seemed so different from what everyone else practiced as Christians. But that burden also proved to be an advantage. It added to an individual's distinct Mormon identity. Moreover, Joseph made it very clear that the Mormon identity was different from that of Protestants, for it was not his purpose to reform Christianity, like Protestant churches. Rather, he had come to restore what was ancient and lost, restore the teachings and institutions of the Savior, restore the doctrines and practices of the New Testament Church.

As the missionary work progressed, Joseph shuttled between groups of believers in Harmony, Pennsylvania (where he and Emma continued to live), and Manchester, Fayette, and Colesville, New York. Wherever he preached he drew increasingly large crowds. The success Joseph enjoyed in proselytizing inevitably aroused the concern of clergymen of other faiths. They accused him of preaching blasphemy and consorting with the devil. He and his family were condemned as "wicked." As William Smith later said, "We never knew we were bad folks until Joseph had his vision. We were considered respectable til then, but at once people began to circulate falsehoods and stories in wonderful ways."

During this period of mounting attention and hostility toward Mormonism, Joseph was distracted by problems at home. Emma was pregnant again and beginning to show signs of stress growing out of their continued poverty and the hostility of neighbors and their clergy. She had endured the outrage and anger of her family and now she worried about Joseph's safety and her own. She may even have had doubts about his mission. In a special revelation to Joseph in July 1830, as reported by him, the Lord admonished her: "Murmur not because of the things which thou has not seen, for they are withheld from thee and from the world." She was to provide "comfort unto my servant, Joseph . . . with consoling words, in the spirit of meekness." She was not to worry because her husband would "support thee from the church." She was also to write and expound scriptures and select hymns for the Church. Dutifully she complied with the command and gathered together ninety hymns, which became the first hymnal of the Church. Apparently the admonition quieted her fears and anxieties and thereafter she believed completely in Joseph's calling.

Not only did the Prophet face criticism and hostility from clergymen of other faiths and their followers, but his own converts sometimes added to his problems. Like Joseph, several of them claimed to have revelations and sought recognition of them from the Church. Oliver Cowdery, David and Peter Whitmer, and Hiram Page had separate revelations, and each felt he had the right to correct Joseph's so-called mistakes. For example, Oliver Cowdery told Joseph that the revelation dealing with the organization of the Church had been transcribed in error. "I command you in the name of God to erase those words," Cowdery insisted, "that no priestcraft be amongst us." Joseph eventually convinced Cowdery and the Whitmers of their own errors, but Page proved intractable. It seems that Page had obtained a seerstone through which he claimed to have received two revelations concerning the "upbuilding of Zion." But Joseph fired back with a new revelation that denied Page's authority to promulgate anything for the Church. Furthermore, what Page had said contradicted the "order of Gods house, as laid down in the new Testament." At a conference of the Church on September 1, 1830, the group unanimously renounced Page's seerstone "and all things connected therewith," and the Prophet "was appointed by the voice of the conference to receive and write Revelations and Commandments for the Church."

Without question this action placed Joseph squarely at the head of the Mormon Church. If there had been any doubt, it existed no longer. In effect he was Moses, who would receive commandments and revelations; Cowdery was Aaron, who would declare them. Only the Prophet could receive scripture and, for good measure, another revelation instructed Cowdery never again to command Joseph "who is at thy head, and at the head of the church" because only Joseph held the "keys of the mysteries, and the revelations."

Here was a remarkable example of Joseph's ability to take command, control events, and lead his followers. There would be future schisms within the Church, but Joseph showed at this early period that he had the capability of withstanding both internal and external attacks on his truthfulness, leadership, and role as the prophet and apostle of Jesus Christ.

In a separate revelation to Joseph, the conference was directed to dispatch a mission to the Indians in the west. Cowdery would head the mission, preaching to the Lamanites, the Lemuelites, and the Ishmaelites and building a temple of God in the "glorious New Jerusalem." This city is mentioned in Revelation in the New Testament of the Bible but is given greater specificity in *The Book of Mormon*. When Christ returned to America after His resurrection, He described a future time and site where the descendants of Jacob would build a city to be called New Jerusalem, a place where all God's scattered people could gather. In time this in-gathering would become a distinguishing feature of the Mormon Church, for the city would provide protection against the terrors to be unleashed at the time of Christ's Second Coming.

Another revelation stated that this city of Zion "shall be on the borders of the Lamanites." The conference leaders knew that the border of Indian country lay on the western edges of Missouri where Native Americans were being removed from their eastern lands and sent west under the terms of the Indian Removal Act, passed by Congress and signed by President Jackson on May 28, 1830. Sending Cowdery off on this Indian mission not only got rid of a possible troublemaker in New

York and placed him in the wilderness hundreds of miles away where he could cause the least internal discord, but also gave him a leadership role that he desperately wanted. He was accompanied by Peter Whitmer Jr., Parley Pratt, and Ziba Peterson, and together they headed west to inaugurate this New Jerusalem.

They left in the fall of 1830 and stopped off at Kirtland, Ohio, a small town east of Cleveland, on their way to the Indian territory. They spent a good deal of time spreading the word of the Restored Gospel and the in-gathering that would take place in New Jerusalem. They preached that God had raised up a prophet and restored the priesthood. They testified to the truth of *The Book of Mormon,* which they distributed; and they succeeded in establishing a branch of twenty or thirty converts. They then wrote a letter to Joseph asking him to send an elder to preside over the branch. Joseph responded by authorizing John Whitmer to take charge of the Kirtland Church; when Whitmer arrived, the Lamanite missionaries renewed their journey and headed for Missouri, "preaching and baptizing as before."

One sympathetic listener to the teaching of Cowdery and his group was Sidney Rigdon, a Baptist minister, a former associate of Alexander Campbell, and an outstanding orator. Tall, handsome, thirty-seven years of age, he was a very emotional man, given to "nervous spasms and swoonings" that he attributed to the Holy Ghost. After hearing Cowdery and Pratt, he and a large number of his congregation were converted to the new religion, after which he decided to go to New York and meet the Prophet in person.

The two men hit it off quite well, and Rigdon received a revelation that like John the Baptist he had been sent to prepare the way. He was also told that Joseph had been given "the fulness of my gospel" and that he, Rigdon, was to watch over the Prophet, "write for him, and the scriptures shall be given." Having worked himself deeply into Joseph's affections, Rigdon moved quite rapidly up the Mormon hierarchy and was ordained an elder of the Church. In time he had "more influence over" Joseph, said David Whitmer, "than any man living. He was Brother Joseph's private counselor and his most intimate friend and brother for some time after they met."

Together these two men visited the Mormon communities in the several surrounding towns. Rigdon electrified his audiences with the power of his personal commitment and articulation of Mormon belief. But this increasing success only activated all the old jealousy and hatred among nonbelievers, whose religious faiths Joseph had condemned as "abominations in the sight of God." By this time the hostility of other churches was reaching a critical mass, making life in New York extremely uncertain and hazardous. This, plus a letter of John Whitmer requesting Joseph's presence in Kirtland and the urging of Sidney Rigdon, convinced Joseph to head west. But first he asked the Lord's guidance. Straightaway he received a revelation commanding him and the entire Church "to go to the Ohio." There they would wait until the Lamanite missionaries in Missouri sent word of the founding of New Jerusalem.

In the meantime, at the conference held on January 2, 1831, it was revealed through Joseph that the lives of his followers were in great jeopardy. "For this cause I gave unto you the commandment that ye should go to the Ohio." There they would begin the gathering of Israel. "There I will give unto you my law, and there you shall be endowed with power from on high." From this sanctuary in Ohio, missionaries should "go forth among all nations" and "you shall be a free people, and ye shall have no laws but my laws when I come."

Accordingly, in late January 1831, an advance party of Latter-day Saints prepared to depart for a land that the Lord promised would be "flowing with milk and honey, upon which there shall be no curse. . . . And I will give it unto you for the land of your inheritance. . . . And they that have farms that cannot be sold, let them be left or rented as seemeth them good." Rigdon delivered an open-air sermon on the steps of the courthouse in Waterloo to a large crowd of believers and nonbelievers, warning them of the dangers to come in New York and the need to flee from the impending disaster.

And so the exodus began. This was the first westward migration of the Mormon Church, a journey of three hundred miles, and it was done in stages. Some waited until the worst of the winter season had passed, but Joseph and Emma, together with Rigdon and Edward Partridge, left New York early on and reached Kirtland around the first of February. A large group from Colesville, supervised by Newel Knight and Joseph Knight Jr., took off in April. Not much later Lucy Smith shepherded a party of fifty aboard a boat on the Cayuga and Seneca Canal, followed in early May by a group of thirty Saints from Waterloo and fifty others from Palmyra. The members sold their property for the best price they could get. As Newel Knight said, "we were obliged to make great sacrifices."

By June 1831 most of the early converts had left New York, knowing they were abandoning their former lives, their farms, their professions, even members of their family. They left behind the historic sites of their newfound faith: the Smith homestead, Hill Cumorah, and the Whitmer farm where the Church had been organized. But they believed they were under the direction of the Lord and were headed for a place where they could find peace and safety.

Chapter 6

Kirtland

NEARLY ONE HUNDRED converts, most of whom had been disciples of Rigdon, were waiting for Joseph when he and Emma arrived in Kirtland. "I am Joseph the Prophet," he boldly announced to Newel K. Whitney, a storekeeper in Kirtland, as they shook hands. "You've prayed me here, now what do you want of me?"

It was an auspicious beginning. Joseph quickly settled in and assumed control of the Kirtland Church. About this time he also began the serious business of translating and revising portions of the King James Bible, particularly those sections which, he said, contained errors or had been lost before they were compiled or had been incorrectly translated. As someone who professed to speak regularly and directly with God, the Prophet felt he had both the right and the duty to undertake this task since important points touching on the salvation of the human race were involved.

Rigdon assisted in the operation. He translated while Joseph revealed. Quite often they claimed they were overpowered by the presence of the Holy Ghost. Joseph would say, "What do I see?" and then describe what he was looking at. Whereupon Rigdon would reply, "I see the same." Or they would reverse roles and Rigdon would describe what he saw and Joseph would exclaim that he saw it too. During these sessions the Prophet would sit "calmly and firmly" in the midst of "a magnificent glory," but poor Rigdon, it was reported, would fall limp and pale from the exaltation. "Sidney is not used to it as I am," Joseph wryly commented.

While he was translating the Gospel of John, it occurred to Joseph that "the Saints' eternal home must include more kingdoms than one," since everyone is rewarded according to his or her merit. Whereupon Joseph and Rigdon learned through another revelation, they said, that there were three kingdoms in heaven, or "three degrees of glory." Those who believed in Christ and kept the commandments would go to the highest or "celestial" kingdom and "dwell in the presence of God and his Christ forever and ever"; those who did not believe in Christ and accept the Gospel, but were "honorable" in life, would go to the "terrestial" kingdom, a lesser state of glory; and those who were wicked, like liars, "adulterers and whoremongers," would go to the "telestial" kingdom until Christ redeemed them at the last resurrection. Only those who denied the Holy Spirit after knowing it and gave themselves to Satan would be cast into hell. Thus, Mormons feel their faith provides a more forgiving Godhead compared with the God of other Christian faiths.

Joseph had actually begun the task of revising the Bible earlier in New York when he revealed a conversation between God and Moses that had been omitted in the Old Testament. This Book of Moses, later published along with other materials as *The Pearl of Great Price,* told of a confrontation between Satan and Moses and of God's determination to bring about the "immortality and eternal life of man." The Book also explained creation, how Satan became the devil and led Adam and Eve into sin, and other events that paralleled those of Genesis. The longest section dealt with the life of Enoch, who gathered a people and built a city called Zion. Because of its intrinsic goodness this city was taken up to heaven but would one day descend to unite in the last days with another Zion, called the New Jerusalem, to be built by a people gathered together from all corners of the earth.*

The idea of gathering believers in New Jerusalem is another example of the profound influence the Jacksonian era had upon Joseph and the development of his Church. Communitarianism was rampant in antebellum America. A number of experiments in communal living emerged at this time in an effort to create new economic patterns for the participants. Some of these had a religious base, while others were essentially nonsectarian. The most famous of the latter was New Harmony in Indiana, established in 1825 by Robert Owen, the Scottish manufacturer and humanitarian. Through collective ownership of property and cooperative labor he hoped to bring about political and economic equality and create a society devoid of crime and poverty. "Who can even imagine," he wrote, "the change it will produce throughout society? The world has never yet seen a republic of cultivated freemen, but the next generation will see it." Unfortunately his advocacy of "free love" and atheism turned many away and eventually his community failed. But the basic idea had widespread appeal and others set about establishing similar operations. For example, the Oneida Community, established in 1848 by John Humphrey Noyes in Seneca Falls, New York, emphasized manufactures rather than agriculture. A divinity student, Noyes attracted more than two hundred followers, who produced such excellent silverware and steel products that the Oneida

---

*The Pearl of Great Price is regarded as scripture by the Mormons who later migrated to Utah, but not by the Mormons who remained in the east and called themselves the Reorganized Church of Jesus Christ of Latter-day Saints.

trademark continues to this day. A third nonsectarian experiment was formed in West Roxbury, Massachusetts, in 1841 by New England intellectuals. Brook Farm, as it was called, lured such literary lights as Nathaniel Hawthorne, Orestes Brownson, Bronson Alcott, and Ralph Waldo Emerson, but a disastrous fire in 1847 destroyed the farm.

The religious experiments in communal living were usually millennialists, such as the Shakers and the Millerites. William Miller of New York, after a careful study of the Bible, predicted the Second Coming on October 22, 1844, at which time all true believers would ascend bodily into heaven. Although the prediction proved mistaken, this sect later evolved into the Seventh Day Adventists.

The Mormons were also millennialists, but Joseph never set an exact date for the Second Coming. He did, however, emphasize the imminent destruction of the world and regularly referred to "these last days." It has been suggested that Sidney Rigdon, having absorbed much of the excitement in the country over Robert Owen's New Harmony, may have put the idea of establishing a similar community in the Prophet's head. Whether this is true or not, it was Joseph who inaugurated a system of "consecration" for the Saints, that is, a sharing of all property among the members to help care for the needy. In effect all private property really became Church property. Converts would consecrate their holdings to the Church and receive back an "inheritance" from the common treasury to enable them to care for themselves and their families. The land would be worked in stewardship, with the surplus to be given to the bishop (a new office Joseph instituted after a series of revelations), who would preside over the community, have charge of temporal affairs, and distribute the surplus among the poor. In theory, then, no one would lack property. All would have an inheritance.

Wisely, Joseph began his experiment in communal living slowly, starting first with the Mormons who followed him from New York and whom he settled in Thompson, adjacent to Kirtland. They were presided over by Newel Knight. The well-established Kirtland Mormons were not included in this initial undertaking. Joseph appointed Edward Partridge bishop, with complete control over buying land and other property, building churches and schools, appointing stewards to judge the needs of converts in allocating land, caring for the poor and aged, and distributing any surplus collected at harvest. There would be two bishops: one for Ohio and the other for the brethren in Missouri.

The notion of gathering the faithful into a community was further emphasized in a revelation of March 7, 1831: "I the Lord, have said, gather ye out from the eastern lands, assemble ye yourselves together ye elders of my church; go ye forth into the western countries . . . build up churches unto me. And with one heart and with one mind gather up your riches that ye may purchase an inheritance which shall hereafter be appointed unto you. And it shall be called the New Jerusalem, a land of peace, a city of refuge, a place of safety for the saints of the Most High God."

And converts came by the dozens, arriving in Kirtland each month, many of them destitute and in need of immediate help. Brigham Young was one of these new arrivals. Born in Whitingham, Vermont, on June 1, 1801, he was a young man in his early thirties, heavyset and rather striking in appearance. After moving to New York with his first wife and reading *The Book of Mormon* shortly after it was published, he was converted and baptized. He left his carpentry business and led a group of converts to Kirtland, where he met Joseph. "My joy was full at the privilege of shaking the hand of the Prophet of God," he said, "and receiving the sure testimony, by the spirit of prophecy, that he was all that any man could believe him to be as a true prophet." Which sums up the way most converts felt about their leader.

Joseph greeted as many of the new arrivals as possible, shaking hands with them and welcoming them into the fold. Gregarious and charming to a fault, he tried to meet and get to know by name and occupation all the new converts to his Church. Indeed, he made every effort to influence, if not control, all aspects of his followers' lives—from what they wore to what they ate and drank to what they believed as Christian doctrine.

On February 4, 1831, he had another revelation, which instructed the Saints to erect a house for the Prophet where he could live and continue the work God had assigned him. In response Isaac Morley built a cabin on his property for the Smiths to live in. A short time later, on April 30, 1831, Emma gave birth to twins, a boy and a girl. Unfortunately they died within a few hours. So devastated were the parents that a pair of nine-day-old twins was presented to them for adoption. Julia and Joseph Murdock, whose mother had died in childbirth, were raised by the Prophet and his wife as their own.

During the next several years, as his congregation grew, Joseph continued adding new offices in the operation of the Church. In the many revelations reported by him during his early years in Ohio—there were sixty-five between 1831 and 1837—most involved the organization, operation, and discipline of the Church. The office of high priest in the Melchizedek priesthood was instituted in 1831, with Joseph as the presiding

High Priest; a year later he chose two counselors to assist him, initiating what became the First Presidency (the word shows another American influence), with supreme authority over all matters concerning the Church. Then in 1833 the office of patriarch was established, a position often held today by older men of proven faith and understanding of the tenets of Mormonism. It corresponds to the ancient office of evangelist. Joseph Smith Sr. was ordained the first Church patriarch on December 18.

Initially the Church had no need for a complex organizational structure, but with increased membership over the following years that situation changed. Again demonstrating remarkable administrative skill, the Prophet directed the formation of the first "stake" on February 17, 1834, presided over by the Prophet and his counselors in the First Presidency. The word comes from a command of the risen Jesus in *The Book of Mormon* to "enlarge the place of thy tent . . . and strengthen thy stakes." The stake serves as the intermediate governing unit between individual communities (later designated as wards), which are local geographical subdivisions to which most Mormons belong, and the ruling authority of the Church at the top. In 1834 two stakes were established, one in Ohio, the other in Missouri, and were led by a three-man stake presidency and a twelve-member high council. High councils arbitrate disputes and take whatever disciplinary action is necessary. Today stakes usually comprise between five and twelve wards or congregations, depending on the number of members, and may cover just a small part of a city or include thousands of towns spread over hundreds of miles. In general a stake brings together members of several communities or wards for instructional and spiritual purposes, installs the leadership of each ward, and maintains Church discipline. In effect it runs the

Church within its boundaries and supervises the activities of bishops. Outside the boundaries of stakes, members are clustered into isolated branches and are led by elders or priests. By 1840 there were eleven stakes in Ohio, Missouri, and Illinois.

It should be emphasized that this organizational structure evolved over a period of years. Wards, for example, were not instituted until 1839. (The term was borrowed from the Illinois political structure.) Today a ward numbers about three hundred to six hundred people. An individual bishop presides over each ward, and he has two counselors to assist him. Bishops serve as pastors and attend to the spiritual, physical, and emotional needs of the members, but most especially their temporal well-being. And they serve without pay.

On February 14, 1835, as a result of several revelations, Joseph organized the Quorum of the Twelve Apostles and two weeks later the Quorum of the Seventy. The former, operating under the direction of the First Presidency, serves as a traveling high council to further the missionary work of the Church, and the Quorum of the Seventy serves under the Twelve. In 1844 Joseph organized the secret Council of Fifty, which is the political arm of the Church.* His revelations instituting these additions, along with others—a total of 138 revelations—were finally published in 1835 as *Doctrine and Covenants.*

The year following the publication of the *Doctrine and Covenants,* further keys of the priesthood were restored to Joseph, or so he said, through the visitations of Moses, Elias, and Elijah, with the command to gather the scattered parts of

---

*Today the First Presidency, the Twelve, the Seventy, and the Presiding Bishopric (a position formed in 1847 after Joseph's death that manages Church properties) constitute the General Authorities of the Church and as a group are referred to as "the Brethren." They represent the highest level of authority in the modern Mormon Church.

Israel into the Church. In addition, sealing powers were conferred by which families, both living and dead, could be linked for eternity, a celebration consecrated in temples. These keys provide the impetus for family history and genealogy, for which the Mormons have become quite well known.

In 1833 Smith founded the School of the Prophets to prepare missionaries for bringing the Restored Church and the Restored Gospel to seekers across the nation and abroad. The completion of Church organization in Joseph's lifetime occurred on March 17, 1842, when Joseph formed the Female Relief Society as a counterpart to the priesthood for men.

Before promulgating the revelations he received, Joseph regularly consulted with the elders. They met in a room over his kitchen, but after each meeting Emma complained to her husband that the floor was covered with spit that she had to clean. The Prophet thought about it, and asked the Lord for guidance. The result was called "The Word of Wisdom," the most important revelation by which Joseph influenced the daily lives of his followers. In it he decreed that Church members should abstain from the use of strong drink, wine, tobacco, and hot drinks, which were believed to be coffee and tea. "That inasmuch as any man drinketh wine or strong drink among you, behold it is not good, neither meet in the sight of your Father. . . . And all saints who remember to do and keep these sayings, walking in obedience to the commandments, shall receive health in their navel and marrow of their bones. And shall find wisdom and great treasures of knowledge, even hidden treasures." The revelation also stressed the need to eat fruit, vegetables, grains, and less meat. In part Joseph was obviously influenced by the rising activities of the Temperance Union, whose membership, beginning in 1826, grew into the millions and which agitated for total abstinence from all alcoholic beverages. Today Mormons are very strict about the use of liquor and other strong drinks, and temperance has become a means of judging the good standing of Church members.

Just as he struggled to give form and structure to his emerging Church, Joseph needed to shape Mormon doctrine into a cohesive and coherent whole. Frequently the Saints were asked about their beliefs. Were they Christian? After all, they were called Mormons, not Christians. Did they believe that Christ was the Lord and Savior? Did they believe in the doctrines of love preached by Christ in the Gospels? Joseph himself was asked so many times about Mormon belief that toward the end of his life, in response to one newspaper editor's query, he decided to provide the world of Gentiles with the basic tenets of the Mormon faith.

"We believe in God, the Eternal Father, and in His Son, Jesus Christ, and in the Holy Ghost," he wrote on March 1, 1842; that through the atonement of Christ all humans can be saved by obedience to the laws and ordinances of the Gospels. "We believe that the first principal and ordinances of the Gospels are: first, faith in the Lord Jesus Christ; second, Repentance; third, Baptism by immersion for the remission of sins; fourth, Laying on of hands for the gift of the Holy Ghost." We also believe that humans will be punished for their sins, not for Adam's transgression. Furthermore, "we believe the Bible to be the word of God, as far as it is translated correctly; we also believe the Book of Mormon to be the word of God." And we believe in an ever-revealing Godhead—a cardinal doctrine that distinguishes the Mormon faith from many other Christian denominations. "We believe," Joseph wrote, "all that God has revealed, all that He now does reveal, and we believe that He will yet reveal great and important things pertaining to the kingdom of God." In other words, God did not stop speaking to His people in biblical times; He has spoken, is still speaking, and will continue to speak and reveal His will and wishes. Through prophets of old, said Joseph, and through prophets of the present and future, the Lord continues to explain the ways of salvation.

Continuing, Joseph declared that Mormons believe "in the literal gathering of Israel and the restoration of the Ten Tribes; that Zion will be rebuilt upon this [American] continent; that Christ will reign personally upon the earth; and that the earth will be renewed and receive its paradisiacal glory." Mormons today profess their belief that through Joseph the ancient Church of Christ and His Gospel were restored and that it exists today as the Church of Jesus Christ of Latter-day Saints, and no other.

Joseph concluded his catalogue by affirming freedom of conscience, obedience to lawful temporal authority, and "in being honest, true, chaste, benevolent, virtuous, and in doing good to *all men.*"

Other important teachings of Joseph resulted from his purchase in July 1835 of four Egyptian mummies and some papyri for $2,400 from a traveling "entrepreneur" by the name of Michael H. Chandler. He then translated the papyri, which contained, he said, writings of the patriarch Abraham. This Book of Abraham became part of *The Pearl of Great Price*, along with the Book of Moses and other writings.

For the most part, the story in the Book of Abraham parallels Genesis and tells how the "Gods organized and formed the heavens and the earth." Notice it is the "Gods," not God, and they "organized," not created, the world out of existing eternal matter. Joseph had decided on the plurality of God because he learned that the Hebrew word *Elohim,* one of the Hebraic words for God, is plural.* In perhaps the greatest sermon Joseph ever preached, a commemorative oration on April 7, 1844, for a Church member by the name of King Follett, who had died in an accident, he elaborated on the doctrine. "In the beginning, the head of the Gods called a council of the Gods; and they came together and concocted a plan" to organize the world and people it. Therefore, Joseph taught, "You have got to learn how to be Gods yourselves . . . the same as all Gods have done before you." And you do it by going step by step from "one small degree to another," gaining wisdom and righteousness and obeying the commandments, until "you are able to dwell in everlasting burnings and to sit in glory."

In this same discourse Joseph also preached that God, as generally understood by Christians, has the physical shape of a man, that the Father and Son are tangible beings of form and substance with whom "we may converse . . . as one man converses with another." In other words, God "has a body of flesh and bones as tangible as man's." In fact He "was once a man like us; yea, that God himself the Father of us all, dwelt on an earth the same as Jesus Christ himself did." He passed through a stage of mortality, just like humans, but he was only one in a succession of gods who did the same. For example, Abraham, Isaac, and Jacob, who once inhabited the earth, are now resurrected beings who have become gods. Later, Lorenzo Snow, the fifth President of the Church, put the doctrine very succinctly in this aphorism: "As man now is, God once was: As God now is, man may be." Joseph also taught that the "intelligence which man possesses is coequal with God himself."

*Many scholars regard the word as an "intensifier" to accent the magnitude of God, not a plural noun.

These radically new doctrines were a far cry from traditional Christianity. They strikingly demonstrate the uniqueness of the Mormon religion.

The Book of Abraham, when finally published in 1842, also related how Abraham insisted on his right of appointment as High Priest, claiming that the Pharaoh of Egypt, a good and decent man, was a descendant of Ham and therefore could not hold the priesthood. That statement later justified Church policy of denying the priesthood to African-Americans, since they supposedly descended from Ham, a policy that continued until 1978, when it was terminated.

In concluding what came to be known as the King Follett Discourse, Joseph made a rather startling statement: "You don't know me; you never knew my heart. No man knows my history; I cannot tell it; I shall never undertake it. I don't blame any one for not believing my history. If I had not experienced what I have, I could not have believed it myself."

Indeed, it was not always easy for his followers to accept some of the revelations Joseph allegedly received at this time. Those who rejected his teaching departed. Others tried to organize resistance within the Church. One revelation that especially troubled some Saints was the one that instituted the system of consecration. Opposition to it forced Joseph to suspend it and substitute a system of tithes. This change came about in a revelation in which the Lord said, "I require all their [the Saints'] surplus property to be put into the hands of the bishop" and then give as tithing one-tenth of their interest or increase annually. "And this shall be a standing law unto them forever, for my holy priesthood, saith the Lord." Bishops had the responsibility of collecting the tithe in each ward and forwarding it to Church headquarters, where the First Presidency and the Quorum of the Twelve Apostles distributed it to fund the work of the Church. Today Mormons are expected to contribute a tenth of their income.

Early in his residence in Kirtland, along with revising the Bible and supervising the Church, Joseph announced publicly that he had been directed by the Lord to go to Missouri and organize a new community, a holy city to be called Zion. In establishing this city he would take with him thirty men, including Rigdon, Martin Harris, and Edward Partridge. After months of preparation the company took off on June 19, 1831, traveling first by wagons, then by canal boats and stages to Cincinnati, and finally by steamer down the Ohio River and up the Mississippi to St. Louis, Missouri. For the remainder of the trip they reportedly walked in the broiling sun across the entire state to Independence in Jackson County. They arrived about the middle of July. Joseph reported that the greeting he received from converts at Independence "was a glorious one and moistened with many tears." Negroes, Indians, and a group of scruffy-looking white frontiersmen and women attended the first meeting he held. A little discouraged by the primitiveness of the area, the Prophet nonetheless gave an impassioned sermon and baptized two converts.

On August 2 he assisted in laying "the first log for a house as a foundation of Zion," at a place about twelve miles west of Independence that later became Kansas City. Twelve men, in honor of the twelve tribes of Israel, carried the log and placed it in position. At the same time the land was consecrated as Zion and dedicated for the gathering of the Saints of the Latter-day. Twenty-four hours later, in a moving ceremony, Joseph blessed the spot for the temple and helped lay the cornerstone.

The first conference in Zion was held on August 4, 1831. Four days later the Prophet had a revelation instructing him to return to Kirtland. The following day Joseph and ten elders, in-

cluding Rigdon, Oliver Cowdery, and William Phelps, returned to Kirtland, leaving Edward Partridge behind to serve
as bishop.

For the next seven years Joseph and other Church elders
shuttled back and forth between the stakes of Ohio and Missouri to deal with both internal and external problems, and he
even went proselytizing in Canada on two occasions, once in
October 1833 and again in August 1837.

Meanwhile a lively Mormon environment developed in
Ohio with the establishment of a newspaper and a press to
provide books and pamphlets for the Church. The brethren
built schools, improved their farms, and began a variety of
commercial ventures. The School of the Prophets offered a
certain amount of education, especially involving missionary
work, and many elders, along with their Prophet, studied Hebrew. What was inaugurated, in fact, was a distinctly Mormon
culture based on the centrality of the Church in the lives of the
Saints; strong family relationships; cooperation and assistance
among the brethren, both economically and spiritually; hard
work; and a determination to build the City of Zion. But these
exciting developments only added to the growing resentment
of non-Mormons in Kirtland.

The increased number of revelations to Joseph about the
activities and conduct of his congregation, giving him even
greater authority over them, and the many Mormons pouring
into the town had so alarmed the Kirtland community that
they generated renewed agitation against the Prophet and his
followers. The poverty of some of the arriving Mormons
brought fears and complaints that they would become "an insupportable weight of pauperism." Moreover, because Mormons tended to act and vote as a bloc, patronizing their own
and boycotting all others, their growing numbers constituted a

threat to the existing economic and political power structure of the town.

The antagonism finally erupted into violence. Late on the night of March 24, 1832, while Joseph watched over one of the twins who was ill with measles, a mob of about forty or fifty men composed of Campbellites, Methodists, Baptists, and apostate Mormons, led by Simonds Ryder, broke into his house, intent perhaps on killing him.

Emma screamed her alarm: "Murder!"

But before the Prophet realized what was happening he was dragged outside and stripped. "I made a desperate struggle, as I was forced out, to extricate myself," Joseph later reported, "but only cleared one leg, with which I made a pass at one man, and he fell on the door steps," his nose bleeding. The attackers "swore by G-d" that they would kill him if he did not stop his struggle. That warning quieted the Prophet, whereupon the man whom he had kicked came up to him and struck him in the face. The man's hand was covered with blood from his own bleeding nose and "with an exulting horse laugh, muttered, '*Ge, gee, G—d—ye, I'll fix ye.*'"

Joseph begged for mercy. Spare my life, he pleaded.

"G—d—ye," the mob responded, "call on yer God for help, we'll show ye no mercy."

Then they tarred and feathered him.

"*Let us tar up his mouth,*" someone cried. At that they tried to force the tar paddle into Joseph's mouth, but he twisted his head away. They tried prying a glass vial of tar into his mouth but he smashed it with his teeth. Finally, their rage assuaged, the mob withdrew, leaving him naked, bruised, covered with tar, and nearly unconscious.

He wiped the tar from his lips so he could breathe and after a few minutes he rose from the ground and dragged himself back to the house. When he got to the door Emma took one look and fainted. In the dark she thought the blotches of tar covering him looked like blood. His friends spent the night scraping the tar from his body and washing him so that by morning he was able to dress himself.

Rigdon, too, was seized, beaten, and dragged by the heels from his home, bumping his head repeatedly on the frozen ground, an assault that left him delirious for days afterward.

Since the following morning was Sunday, the Mormons assembled at the usual hour of worship, and among them were several men who had tarred him the night before, including Simonds Ryder, cynically expecting the Prophet to cancel his appearance. But Joseph surprised them. Despite his pain and with his flesh "all scarified and defaced," he walked boldly into the hall. Then, with the true instinct of an actor and consummate spiritual leader, he preached as usual, never once paying a bit of attention to his attackers. His performance under the circumstances greatly increased his already heroic stature among the Saints.

To add to the family's suffering, Joseph Murdoch Smith, the twin who had been ill with measles, grew worse in the following days and died on March 29, 1832, leaving only one child to the Smiths, Julia Murdoch. Fortunately, on November 6, 1832, Emma bore another child, this time a son, who was given his father's name.

A month prior to the birth of Joseph Smith III, the Prophet sent Emma to live with the Whitney family in Kirtland while he undertook a trip to Albany, New York, and Boston, where he and Newel Whitney negotiated loans and bought dry goods for a general store that Joseph planned to open in Kirtland. While in New York he heard that South Carolina had nullified the nation's tariff laws and had threatened to secede from the Union if military force was used against her. On December 10, 1832, President Jackson issued a proclamation to the people of South Carolina and warned them that "disunion by armed force is *treason*. Are you really ready to incur its guilt?" And he made it quite clear that he was prepared to initiate a bloody conflict if the state did not rescind its Ordinance of Nullification.

Two weeks later, on Christmas Day 1832, Joseph had another revelation in which he foretold that war would "shortly come to pass, beginning at the rebellion of South Carolina, which will eventually terminate in the death and misery of many souls. . . . For behold, the Southern States shall be divided against the Northern States, and the Southern States will call on other nations, even the nation of Great Britain . . . in order to defend themselves. . . . And it shall come to pass, after many days, slaves shall rise up against their masters, who shall be marshaled and disciplined for war."

The crisis in 1832 with South Carolina was quickly resolved with the passage of the Compromise Tariff of 1833, arranged by Henry Clay and John C. Calhoun. Once the compromise was agreed upon, South Carolina rescinded its Nullification Ordinance. But several decades later Joseph's prophecy became reality. It was a prediction that any number of other people made at the time, including Clay, Calhoun, and Daniel Webster.

One of the most important revelations Joseph received during his Ohio residence came on June 1, 1833, when God allegedly instructed him to build a temple in Kirtland where He "could endow those whom I have chosen with power from on high." The precedent was established by Christ when He commanded His apostles to "tarry" in Jerusalem "until ye be endowed." Therefore, said the Lord in His revelation to Joseph, "I command you to tarry, even as mine apostles at Jerusalem." For it was only in a temple that the endowments could be conferred.

A Mormon temple is not simply a church in the usual sense. It is a special place where endowments "of things spiritual" are received "by the spiritual minded" through washings and anointings; regular Sunday services by Mormons are normally held in chapels.

Although many of his people were poor and struggling to survive, Joseph announced that the Lord had commanded them to build a temple and that they must begin at once. "Organize yourselves; prepare every needful thing; and establish a house, even a house of prayer, a house of fasting, a house of faith, a house of learning, a house of glory, a house of order, a house of God." At this time the Church in Kirtland consisted of several hundred individuals, yet all of them pitched in to build the structure. They lived, as one said, "as abstemiously as possible" so that "every cent might be appropriated to the grand object." Lumber was brought from the forests, and stone from a nearby quarry. Joseph also directed the building of a temple in Zion, the Mormon settlement outside Independence, Missouri.

The order to the Missouri stake came at the worst possible time. There the Saints found intense hostility from original settlers who were southern slave owners, which most Mormons were not. When the territory of Missouri, carved out of the Louisiana Purchase, first petitioned to enter the Union as a slave state it provoked a sectional clash in Congress between northerners and southerners. For one thing it would upset the balance of voting strength in the U.S. Senate between free and slave states. In addition it raised the question of whether Congress had the constitutional right to restrict slavery in the territories. Southerners threatened to secede if their right to take their slaves into the territory was jeopardized in any way. The Missouri Compromise of 1820–1821 resolved the crisis when a line was drawn along the 36°30' parallel within the remaining Louisiana territory, with slavery prohibited north of that line. To maintain the voting balance in the Senate, Missouri was admitted as a slave state and Maine, which had been part of Massachusetts, was admitted as a free state.

Having determined that their state would permit slavery, the original settlers of Missouri were not about to allow "outsiders" to come in and alter this decision. They rightly feared that the rapidly increasing numbers of these "deluded fanatics" could mean ultimate Mormon control of the state and the outlawing of slavery. At the very least Mormons would take over local government and run it according to their religious precepts. "The day is not far distant," read one printed and rabidly anti-Mormon "Manifesto," when "the civil government of the county will be in their hands; when the sheriff, the justices, and the county judges will be Mormons, or persons wishing to court their favor from motives of interest or ambition." Another "Manifesto" charged that Mormons "openly blasphemed the Most High God, and cast contempt on His holy religion, by pretending to receive revelations . . . by direct inspiration, and by divers pretenses derogatory of God and religion." The settlers also resented the attitude of these "Yankee" invaders who seemed to think that God had given them this land for their New Jerusalem. Furthermore, the Mormons' sense of community and mutual assistance, the success of their operations in establishing a printing house with a press to "spew their filthy propaganda," their friendliness with the hated and feared Indians whom they attempted to convert, and the fact that they called themselves Saints, as though non-believers were sinners—all this built up a towering hostility against the brethren that finally triggered an explosion in the winter of 1832–1833. Mormon houses were burned, and leaders of the Church were tarred and feathered. The printing house and press were destroyed after issuing a pro-abolitionist article. When the persecution continued through the spring and summer and finally became intolerable, the Saints fled to Clay County in the bitter cold of November 1833. There they found temporary housing in tents, makeshift shelters, and abandoned cabins.

In response to a revelation of February 24, 1834, Joseph led a small army of two hundred followers, including Brigham Young, to Missouri to protect their brethren against further assault. Called Zion's Camp, the expedition collapsed because of dissension in the ranks followed by an outbreak of cholera. Discouraged, this Mormon militia turned around and returned to Kirtland.

For three years the Missouri Mormons enjoyed temporary asylum in Clay County, but then they were unceremoniously informed by local residents that they had to leave. The Saints appealed to the legislature for help, and in response the counties of Caldwell and Daviess, which they might settle, were organized in 1835. The Saints immediately departed from Clay County and moved into Caldwell, a remote area in northern Missouri. There they lived in a true wilderness and called it "Far West."

The temple in Missouri might have to wait awhile before it could be erected, but construction of the temple in Kirtland began on June 23, 1833, with Hyrum Smith declaring "that he would strike the first blow upon the house" by digging a trench for the wall. Some of the elders suggested a frame structure or a log house. But Joseph dismissed those ideas. "Shall we brethren," he said, "build a house for our God, of logs? No, I have a better plan than that." Following the directions given him in a series of revelations, Joseph supervised the building of a two-story structure with an attic, and he patterned its interior after the Tabernacle of Moses and the Temple of Solomon. When finally completed, the interior of the building measured 55 feet wide, 65 feet long, and 110 feet high to the dome of the steeple. Two main floors were used for prayer, preaching, "sacrament offering," fasting, and "offering upon your most holy desires" to the Lord. The attic area was reserved mainly for classrooms to train missionaries.

What arose in Kirtland was a typical New England meetinghouse of the time, combining Federal with Greek Revival features as well as a touch of the Gothic. Money for this grandiose construction had to be begged and borrowed from believers and nonbelievers alike. The ultimate cost came to approximately $50,000, an enormous sum for a people struggling to stay alive. But such devoted Mormons as John Tanner sold their property to help defray the cost. Tanner relinquished two farms and 2,200 acres of timber and loaned the temple committee $13,000. He also signed a note with Joseph for $30,000 worth of goods. Men donated one day of labor a week to the construction, while the women spent their time "knitting, spinning and sewing" and preparing meals for the laborers. The women also contributed their glassware to be crushed and mixed with the plaster, thereby providing a sparkling appearance to the exterior. The work went on even though an increasing chorus of dissent could be heard from some disaffected Mormons who thought the money could be better spent on needy members of the congregation. And militant Kirtland townspeople also got the community worked up over fears of what the swelling numbers of Mormons would mean for the future of local governance. Mormon rule would be Church rule, they contended, and the beginning of a probable theocracy. Such resentment and bitterness prompted the Saints to guard the temple at night and work with a gun in one hand and a trowel in the other during the day.

In addition to temples, Joseph began to design a city with broad streets and avenues laid out in squares, a design Brigham Young would later employ in laying out Salt Lake City. These plans were daring in their scope and purpose and clearly demonstrated the Prophet's growing confidence in his control and leadership and in his vision for the welfare of his people.

The temple was dedicated on Sunday, March 27, 1836, in an atmosphere bordering on religious delirium, with a repeat ceremony on March 31. A thousand worshipers, many of whom had arrived at 7:00 A.M., an hour before the doors were scheduled to open, filled the first-floor auditorium. Another thousand stood outside, and Joseph urged them to go to the schoolhouse and hold a separate service, which they did.

Joseph, Rigdon, and Cowdery seated the congregation as they entered. The First Presidency occupied the pulpit for the Melchizedek priesthood, with the high priests, the Quorum of the Twelve Apostles, the Seventies, and assorted members of the high council, bishops, priests, and teachers stationed at various other points around the hall. The choir was seated in the four corners of the room.

The service began with a prayer and several readings; then came the singing of "The Spirit of God like a Fire Is Burning," followed by a full-throated shout, "Hosanna to God and the Lamb, with an Amen, Amen, Amen." Men said they felt the Holy Ghost like fire in their very being; visions and prophecies were called out, as well as "cursings upon the enimies of Christ who inhabit Jackson county Missouri." This was followed by shouts of Hosanna and Amen.

At 9:00 A.M. Rigdon read the 96th and 24th Psalms; then he spoke for two and half hours, after which he summoned the quorums and the congregation to sustain Joseph as Prophet and Seer. When Joseph finally rose to speak, the atmosphere was explosively charged. He begged the Savior for a visible manifestation as had occurred at Pentecost. "Let thy house be filled with a rushing mighty wind, with thy glory," he implored. Let the grace of God descend upon us. "O Lord God Almighty, hear us in these our petitions, and answer us from heaven." As he spoke he raised his hands toward heaven with "tears running down his cheeks." He concluded his long dedicatory prayer with "O hear, O hear, O hear us O Lord . . . and accept the dedication of this house, unto Thee, the work of our hands, which we have built unto thy name, and also this Church to put upon it Thy name. . . . And help us by the power of Thy spirit . . . and let these Thine anointed ones be clothed with salvation, and thy saints shout aloud for joy. Amen and Amen."

Again the congregation with uplifted hands shouted "Hosannah to God and the Lamb." Once the noise level subsided somewhat, bread and wine were distributed, whereupon Joseph "bore testimony of the administering of angels." Then he "sealed the proceedings of the day by shouting hosannah to God and the lamb 3 times sealing it each time with Amen, Amen, and Amen." By then, he claimed, the temple was filled with angels.

"Brigham Young gave a short address in tongues," interpreted by David W. Patten, after which Joseph blessed the congregation and the members dispersed at 4:00 P.M.

No one can adequately describe "the heavenly manifestations of that memorable day," declared one woman. Hundreds spoke in tongues, others prophesied. Oliver Cowdery insisted that he "saw cloven tongues, like as fire rest upon many." One man testified that at the first prayer an angel entered through the window and sat down beside him. Outside one young girl said she saw "on the temple angels clothed in white covering the roof from end to end. They seemed to be walking to and fro; they appeared and disappeared." Others said they beheld a pillar of fire resting upon the temple.

The dedication continued for an entire week, and on Sunday, April 3, Joseph and Oliver Cowdery, the first and second elder, conducted the concluding service.

They mounted the pulpit. A veil was lowered to conceal their presence while the congregation watched and prayed. Then when the curtain was lifted the Prophet called out, "We have seen the Lord." Jesus, he said, was "standing upon the breast work of the pulpit before them, and under his feet was a paved work of pure gold, in color like amber: his eyes were as a flame of fire; the hair of his head was white like the pure snow, his countenance shone above the brightness of the sun, and his voice was as the sound of the rushing of great waters, even the Voice of Jehovah, saying, I am the first and the last, I am he who liveth, I am he who was slain, I am your Advocate with the Father. Behold, your sins are forgiven you. You are clean before me, therefore, lift up your heads and rejoice, let the hearts of your brethren rejoice. . . . For behold I have accepted this house, and my name shall be here; and I will manifest myself to my people, in mercy, in this House."

The congregation believed all that Joseph told them, and such glad tidings must have sent the congregation into a convulsive state of rapture. But there was more. After this vision closed, said the Prophet, the heavens opened again and Moses appeared and committed to Joseph and Oliver "the keys of the gathering of Israel from the four parts of the Earth and the leading of the ten tribes from the Land of the North." Following Moses came Elias, who "committed the dispensation of the gospel of Abraham" to them. Then Elijah appeared to announce that "the keys of this dispensation are committed into your hands, and by this ye may know that the great and dreadful day of the Lord is near, even at the doors."

The meaning to Mormons of the restoration of these keys to Joseph is that the Church of Latter-day Saints now had divine authority to go forth and build the Kingdom of God on earth in anticipation of the Second Coming.

In the following days and weeks the Saints rejoiced over this manifestation of God's love and commitment to them. There was feasting and prophesying and the dispensing of blessings all around. For Mormons it was one of the supreme moments in their history, and no one who was there ever forgot it. Nothing like it ever happened again.

To add to the general mood of rejoicing in Kirtland at this time, Emma bore a second son, Frederick, on June 20, 1836. Now there were three children in the family: Julia, Joseph III, and Frederick.

But the triumphant moment of the dedication of the temple did not come without internal turmoil within the Mormon community. Resentment over the building of such an extravagant structure lingered among some Saints. Others objected to the "system of consecration." Still others began to have doubts about Joseph himself. Recently attacks had mounted by rivals and enemies who challenged the veracity of his claims and accused him of worldly desires. Even more damaging were scandalous reports of his having committed adultery, particularly with Fanny Alger, a seventeen-year-old hired girl who had been taken into the family. Oliver Cowdery openly accused Joseph of adultery, perhaps because he knew that the principle of plural marriage, which he objected to, had been revealed to Joseph in 1831 and that the Prophet had already taken his first plural wife.* As a matter of fact, Joseph had earlier informed one of the members of the Quorum of the Seventy that the ancient practice of polygamy would be restored. In a letter to his brother, Cowdery labeled Joseph's relations with Fanny as a "dirty, nasty, filthy affair." Polygamy would not be proclaimed publicly until a much later date, and this instance may have been the first stirring of opposition to the principle among some Mormons.

Of course Joseph was an extremely attractive man. His friendliness, his ingratiating manner, his thoughtful consideration of the needs of others, his infectious smile, his beguiling eyes, and his power and influence in the Church drew women to him constantly. "The people fairly adored him," said one. "I am bold to say that, Jesus Christ excepted, no better man ever lived or does live upon this earth," remarked Brigham Young. "I feel like shouting Hallelujah all the time, when I think that I ever knew Joseph Smith, the Prophet."

Even so, disaffection mounted, and the situation in Kirtland seemed to be slipping out of Joseph's control. Some Mormons drifted away from him for one or more reasons. They said he had fallen, that he had betrayed their trust, that he was an infidel. They called him a liar, false prophet, and blasphemer. "Disaffection and apostacy . . . prevailed so extensively," declared Brigham Young, "that it was difficult for any to see

---

*Fanny later moved to Indiana but never confirmed or denied her marriage to Joseph.

clearly the path to pursue. . . . The knees of many of the strongest men in the Church faltered." Ezra Booth, a former Methodist preacher who had converted to Mormonism, became so disillusioned that he denounced the Prophet in a letter to the local newspaper, calling him an impostor and a fraud. Others hauled Joseph into court on one charge or another. In fact, during the week of the dedication ceremonies, Leeman Copley came to him and confessed that he had testified falsely against him and had since repented and asked forgiveness.

Adding fuel to the fire, Joseph undertook an operation that ultimately ended in disaster for him and his Church. Because the number of Mormons had grown substantially over the previous few years, their needs and those of their community had grown as well. The spiraling cost of the increased missionary work undertaken by the Church necessitated a search for loans to pay ever-mounting debts. The Missouri Mormons in Far West were in constant want, and Joseph periodically sent them what money he could scrape together. Finally, in November 1836, he and his advisors decided to establish a bank to help liquidate all their debts.

The Kirtland Safety Society Bank was organized with a capital stock of "not less than four million dollars." Sidney Rigdon was appointed president and Joseph the cashier. Banknotes were issued that quickly circulated among farmers in desperate need of cash. The bank's stock, ranging from one thousand dollars upward, was also snatched up by those who could afford it. Invariably subscribers offered their land at inflated prices for the stock.

The question of banking in the Jacksonian era was very contentious. At the start of his administration President Jackson had insisted on changes in the operation of the federally chartered Second National Bank of the United States (BUS). Congress defied him and passed legislation in 1832 rechartering the BUS four years before the charter was due to expire, whereupon Jackson vetoed the measure. When his veto was sustained and he was elected to a second term, he proceeded to remove the government's deposits from the BUS and place incoming revenues (mainly from federal land sales and tariff duties) in selected state banks, called "pet banks" by his political opposition. With the large surplus he also paid off the national debt in 1835, the first and only time that has happened in the history of the United States.

Joseph picked a particularly bad time to start a bank because wildcat banking had intensified as a consequence of Jackson's Bank War. Therefore, the Ohio legislature, on a crusading mission, refused to charter the Kirtland bank, although Joseph declared that the charter was rejected because the proprietors were Mormons. Then disaster struck. Because of the failure of the New Orleans cotton market, the I. and L. Joseph Company of New York, one of the largest dealers in domestic exchange, toppled into bankruptcy on March 17, 1837. Since it had holdings in a variety of commercial and mercantile enterprises around the country, its failure set off a chain reaction that quickly engulfed the nation. The price of gold and silver soared, and a run on banks and a suspension of specie payments ensued. Over the next several months one bankruptcy followed another and the nation verged on financial collapse.

This Panic of 1837 was one of the most severe to hit the country in its history and lasted over six years. President Jackson had left office by the time it began, replaced by his hand-picked successor, Martin Van Buren. The new administration had hardly begun when the financial catastrophe struck. It brought havoc to the Kirtland bank, which soon closed its doors, leaving many creditors demanding payment and blaming the Prophet for their losses. The bank's notes were worthless, and those who held them cursed Joseph for defrauding them. It has been calculated that for the period 1835–1837 his personal indebtedness reached $100,000. Eventually $60,000 was settled, but that did not keep angry depositors from venting their rage in lawsuits, thirteen of which were ultimately concluded in the Prophet's favor.

Still, the turmoil tore the Mormon community apart. The number of apostates escalated and they became more vocal. Additional lawsuits were instituted, and Mormon meetings frequently ended in near riot. A coup was hatched to overthrow Joseph and replace him as Prophet. At a conference called on September 3, 1837, Joseph tried to heal the breach, but he failed. Under the leadership of Warren Parrish, who had been Joseph's secretary, more than thirty prominent Mormons renounced the Prophet, among them a member of the First Presidency and several of the Twelve, the Seventy, and the high council. Even Oliver Cowdery, David Whitmer, and Martin Harris, the witnesses of *The Book of Mormon,* joined the rebels, believing that Joseph had betrayed the Church.

So turbulent and violent had Kirtland become that "a man's life was in danger the moment he spoke in defence of the Prophet." On December 22, Brigham Young was hounded out of town for daring to declare publicly that Joseph Smith was "a Prophet of the Most High God."

By the end of 1837 the situation had gotten completely out of hand. "The enemy abroad and apostates in our midst united in their schemes," Joseph declared, ". . . and many became disaffected toward me as though I were the sole cause of those very evils I was most strenuously striving against." With mounting lawsuits against him, one of which included an arrest warrant on the charge of fraud, with renewed hostility from other Christian sects, and with the Church racked by dissension, Joseph decided to heed the instruction of Jesus, who said, "when they persecute you in one city, flee to another." On the evening of January 12, 1838, he and Rigdon left Kirtland on horseback "to escape mob violence," he declared, and headed for Far West to join the Saints in northern Missouri. "A new year dawned upon the Church in Kirtland in all the bitterness of the spirit of apostate mobocracy, which continued to rage and grow hotter and hotter," he wrote, "until Elder Rigdon and myself were obliged to flee from its deadly influence, as did the Apostles of old."

And then something quite extraordinary happened. Hundreds of Mormons in Kirtland suddenly realized the enormity of their loss. Those who had revolted controlled the temple but none of them had the presence, the leadership, and the commanding assurances of Joseph. It was he who had given them *The Book of Mormon,* which they believed in and revered. It was he who had restored the Church and the priesthood and held the keys to the new dispensation. Joseph Smith Jr. was the Prophet who would build the New Jerusalem. How could they go on without their founder, their lawgiver? How could there be a Church without him? So in their sudden realization of their tremendous loss, they decided to pack their belongings and join him in Zion. The most radical of the opponents remained disaffected, of course, and there were a fair number of them, but most Kirtland Mormons, probably a majority, shucked off their disappointment in and rancor toward Joseph. They discovered they genuinely loved and revered him and could not continue without him.

That summer a mile-long wagon train formed in Kirtland and headed for Missouri, its passengers leaving behind farms and businesses, the temple, and many friends. Still, these Mormons knew what they had to do. They knew their future rested with their Prophet and lawgiver, Joseph Smith Jr.

Chapter 7

Far West

JOSEPH AND RIGDON joined their families at Norton, in Medina County, Ohio, and pushed on as quickly as possible, since any number of citizens in the communities along the way held banknotes from the Kirtland bank and accosted the Prophet as he rode through their towns. A few even had writs against him. But he escaped prosecution by hiding in the back of Rigdon's wagon. It was a rough journey, not only because of the irate citizens ready to haul him into court, but because of the late winter storms. Despite these problems, he and his family finally arrived in Far West, Caldwell County, Missouri, on March 13, 1838. Eight miles from the settlement they were met by an escort of brethren who received them "with open arms and warm hearts." In town they were greeted, said Joseph, "on Every hand by the Saints . . . to the land of their inheritance." This idea that the land somehow belonged to Mormons as an inheritance did not sit well with other Missourians and was another factor in the escalating tense relationship between the two groups. For nothing causes trouble quicker than a religious community claiming that its property rights have divine authorization.

Still, the welcome was so spontaneous and heartfelt that Joseph felt fully compensated for "our long seven years of Servitude persecution & affliction in the midst of our enimies in the land Kirtland." There were about five thousand Saints in

Far West, and their number would grow with the arrival of hundreds more from Ohio later that summer.

The town had been laid out with wide streets in checkerboard fashion according to the plan suggested earlier by Joseph. He and his family found shelter in the home of George W. Harris, where he said he had nothing to do but attend to his spiritual concerns and the affairs of the Church. And it was here in Far West that Joseph finally declared the official name of his faith to be The Church of Jesus Christ of Latter-day Saints.

In the following months, with the arrival of the Kirtland Saints, Joseph designated a site for a temple and participated in the excommunication of Oliver Cowdery, David and John Whitmer, William W. Phelps, and Lyman E. Johnson on charges of defaming him for his alleged adultery, for his supposed use of liquor and tobacco in violation of "The Word of Wisdom," and for what they said was his dishonesty and demeaning of the Church.* These men had been among his earliest and staunchest supporters. Several of them had led the first contingents of Mormons into Missouri, and both Cowdery and Whitmer had been witnesses to *The Book of Mormon.* Of the original eleven witnesses, two had died and six either had left the Church voluntarily or had been excommunicated. Now only Joseph's father and brothers remained.

Because violent hatred seemed to follow the brethren wherever they went, Joseph encouraged but apparently did not participate in the activities of a newly formed secret society

---

*After a clash with Rigdon and a refusal to join the Kirtland Safety Society Bank, Martin Harris had been excommunicated in December 1837. He later returned to the faith and moved to Utah and was rebaptized.

among Mormons, known as the Sons of Dan, or Danites, founded by Sampson Avard. This clandestine organization, whose members were bound by secret oaths and passwords, constituted a veritable Mormon militia, but one that also participated in public functions such as Fourth of July celebrations. Initially the Danites were intended to defend the First Presidency and ferret out dissenters. In Joseph's Missouri journal, the entry for July 27, 1838, states that "we have a company of Danites in these times, to put to right physically that which is not right, and to cleanse the Church of verry great evils which hath hitherto existed among us inasmuch as they cannot be put to right by teachings and persuasyons." But the activities of Avard's Danites soon widened to include retaliatory strikes against hostile non-Mormons, some of which crossed over into criminal acts, including robbery and the burning of homes and fields. Because Avard treated disloyalty toward the First Presidency as heinous, he had Joseph's full confidence and support at first and became one of the most powerful men in the Church. But it was a brief reign, lasting from June to November 1838. Later, when the crimes committed by the Danites grew more and more violent, the organization was repudiated and Avard himself excommunicated.

But it had clearly become imperative for the Saints to protect themselves against the early settlers of Missouri, who resented their presence and growing economic and political power. These Gentiles "watched our increasing power and prosperity with jealousy," wrote one Mormon, "and with greedy and avaricious eyes. It was a common boast that, as soon as we had completed our extensive improvements, and made a plentiful crop, they would drive us from the State, and once more enrich themselves with the spoils."

This "increasing power and prosperity" of Mormons proved

to be a serious and overriding element in the deteriorating relations between the Saints and the Gentiles. As hardworking and dedicated farmers and businessmen, Mormons understood that only by profitable enterprises could they acquire the necessary means to build Zion. They therefore reached hungrily for "the perishable riches of this world." By achieving economic self-sufficiency and worldly gain—whether by farming or commercial activities—they would not only help advance the work of the Church in all its activities but assist in bringing about the creation of the New Jerusalem.

Such success worsened their already wretched relations with non-Mormons, and the hatred had now become fierce. Mormons, snarled one, are nothing but "a tribe of locusts, that still threatens to scorch and wither the herbage of a fair and goodly portion of Missouri by the swarm of emigrants from their pestilent hive in Ohio and New York." They were nothing more than a "mass of human corruption."

On May 18, 1838, Joseph, Rigdon, and several others headed northward into Daviess County to find additional land and arrange a settlement for the swelling Mormon population. In a revelation to Joseph on May 19, 1838, the place chosen was named Adam-ondi-Ahman.* It was located on the horseshoe bend of the Grand River, twenty-five miles north of Far West, and so named because Joseph said it was the place where Adam shall come to visit his people. It is commonly believed among Mormons that Adam went to this place after he had been expelled from the Garden of Eden and that it will be

---

*According to the *Mormon Encyclopedia,* Orson Pratt, a member of the first Quorum of the Twelve Apostles, interpreted the name to mean "Valley of God, where Adam dwelt."

the site of a future meeting of the Lord with Adam and the Saints, as foretold by the prophet Daniel.

Joseph settled converts from Canada into Adam-ondi-Ahman "as they are emigrating numerously to this land from all parts of the Country." From June to October 1838 their number rose to about four hundred, and they congregated within a two-mile radius of the town. An additional six hundred Mormons occupied Daviess County and regarded Adam-ondi-Ahman as their capital city. The month following its establishment Adam-ondi-Ahman became the third stake of the Church, with John Smith, Joseph's uncle, as stake president. Since the Missouri authorities had not yet put the land up for sale, the Saints occupied it under the right of preemption with the intention of purchasing it once it went on the market. They not only farmed the land but greatly improved it each year of their residence.

The troubled situation in Far West came to full heat when Joseph decided to hold the ceremonies for the laying of the temple's cornerstone on the Fourth of July 1838. By this act he meant to make a public statement about the Mormon presence in Missouri: the brethren would celebrate both their freedom as Americans and "our declaration of independence from all mobs and persecutions which have been inflicted upon us time after time until we can bear it no longer." We have been "driven by ruthless mobs and enimies of the truth from our homes," he declared, "our property confiscated our lives exposed and our all jeopardized by such conduct."

Thousands turned out for the event, including a number of old settlers who may or may not have been looking for trouble. The Danites led the parade. Behind them the Mormons marched triumphantly to the construction site, saluting their brethren as they marched and by their shouts demonstrating their strength and commitment to their Church. It was a spectacle that Joseph had planned for and delighted in. It was a day full of "pomp and glory."

Rigdon gave the principal address in the public square "under the hoisted flagg representing the Liberty and independence of these United States of America." But it proved disastrous. Rigdon was a fire-breathing Mormon who raged at dissenters, critics, enemies of the First Presidency, and anyone who threatened his faith. He threw down the gauntlet to all those who would dare to assault the Church or its members. "Our cheeks have been given to the smiters, and our heads to those who have plucked off the hair," he stormed. "We have not only, when smitten on one cheek, turned the other, but we have done it again, and again, until we are wearied of being smitten, and tired of being trampled upon." He paused and then in measured tones, slowly and deliberately, added, "But from this day and hour, we will suffer it no more."

Surely the brethren in the crowd roared their approval and clapped their hands while the old settlers, stunned at this bold-faced challenge, stood silent.

But Rigdon had not finished his harangue. "And that mob that comes on us to disturb us," he announced, "it shall be between us and them a war of extermination," for we will pursue this course until "the last drop of their blood is spilled, or else they will have to exterminate us."

Extermination! It was something of a battle cry. And he called it that. "We will carry the seat of war to their own houses and their own families" and either they or us "shall be utterly destroyed." We will not be the aggressors, he declared. We will not infringe the rights of any person. But we shall stand up to anyone who persecutes us, and we will stand "until death."

Then, in the full majesty of his oratorical prowess, he thundered, "We this day then proclaim ourselves free, with a purpose and a determination that never can be broken—No never! no never! NO NEVER!!!"

At that, Joseph cried out "Hosannah!" and the crowd erupted with shouts of "Hosanna, hosanna to God and the Lamb."

The non-Mormons could scarcely believe what they had just heard. Unfortunately the speech was published and circulated around the state, and the result was an avalanche of abusive editorials from Missouri newspapers and threatening stump speeches from politicians who were preparing for the state elections on August 6. Mormons were denounced as murderers, thieves, idolaters, blasphemers, and liars. They need to be driven from the state, cried one mob, so that the country can be cleansed of their "filth."

On election day the situation descended into violence when the Mormons decided to exercise their right to vote in Gallatin, the county seat. Seen by local settlers as a voting bloc who could initiate unwanted political changes in the county, the Saints were challenged as they strode to the polls. William Peniston, a Whig candidate for the Missouri House of Representatives who may have feared defeat in the election, vented his anger in the town's square by giving an impromptu speech about how the Mormons would take over everything and deny citizens their legal rights. Liberty itself was at stake, he roared.

A ruffian by the name of Richard Weldon called out that the Mormons had no right to vote, "no more than the damned negroes." Then he struck one of the elders over the head.

That did it. A scuffle ensued and then a general melee as the brethren and locals tore into one another. It was reported that about 150 Missourians joined in the battle, quite a number of whom had their "sculs cracked." Fortunately no one was killed but several Mormons, who "faut like tigers," were wounded in the riot. Thus began the so-called Mormon War of 1838.

News of the disturbance quickly spread, and brethren from the surrounding areas raced to Gallatin. Rigdon summoned all able-bodied Mormons to join in defending the faith. Intermittent fighting continued for the next several days. In an effort to secure their rights a group of Saints went to the local justice of the peace, Adam Black, and insisted that he provide them with a written statement that he would uphold the law and not authorize mob action against them. Black agreed. They then worked out an agreement with some of the leading citizens of the county to preserve the peace and defend the rights of all.

But Peniston had no intention of allowing the disturbance to be forgotten. On August 10 he swore out an affidavit before Circuit Court Judge Austin A. King that Joseph Smith Jr. and Colonel Lyman Wight had led an army of about five hundred men into the county "whose movements and conduct are of a highly insurrectionary and unlawful character." Furthermore, they invaded Adam Black's home and "under threats of immediate death" forced him to sign a "very disgraceful paper." They are now assembled, the affidavit stated, and intend "to commit great violence to many of the citizens of Daviess county." Without a moment's hesitation the judge swore out a writ to apprehend Joseph and Wight and try them for their alleged crimes.

Fearing he would be lynched in Gallatin, Joseph insisted on the right to be tried in his own town, and he was bound over on a five-hundred-dollar bond to keep the peace. But hostility continued to mount. Throughout the countryside men on both sides armed themselves. "The deafening sound of the drum and the din of arms," reported one newspaper, resonated around the state. Armed bands of Missourians terrorized the Saints by burning their homes and farms and fields. They wanted the Mormons out of their county and out of their state. "Mobs began to gather in various places and commenced their hostilities," wrote Joseph Horne. "So much so that we were obliged to shoulder our guns and stand guard night and day."

At this point the governor, Lilburn Boggs, stepped into the conflict and issued the incredible "extermination order" in which he authorized an increase in the size of the militia to undertake the special task of ridding Missouri of Mormons. "The Mormons must be treated as enemies," read the order, "and must be exterminated or driven from the state, if necessary for the public good. Their outrages are beyond all description." Once empowered, the militia soon demonstrated their appetite and capacity for exterminating Mormons. It was open season on the "vermin."

In late October segments of the Missouri militia surrounded a settlement at Haun's Mill and systematically slaughtered Mormon men and boys who tried to flee. Children had their brains blown out at point-blank range and women were assaulted. Seventeen people died and thirteen were wounded. What made it even more painful was the fact that a number of former Mormons had joined the rampaging militia. Thereafter Haun's Mill became a lasting symbol of the bigotry, hatred, and oppression heaped upon all Mormons.

But the Haun's Mill massacre prompted both sides to recognize the need for a truce. A committee was formed, including George Hinkle, who commanded the Mormon forces, which made the arrangements for a "discussion" to be held under a flag of truce between Church elders (including Joseph) and a rabidly anti-Mormon commander of state troops, General Samuel D. Lucas. In what the Prophet later regarded as a betrayal on the part of Hinkle (he called him a "wolf in sheep's clothing"), the supposed meeting became a trap. Lucas promptly arrested and imprisoned Joseph, Hyrum Smith, Rigdon, Wight, and others when they showed up to discuss a truce. As the elders walked into the camp the militiamen "all set up a constant yell like so many bloodhounds let loose upon their prey."

Shackled and loaded into wagons, the prisoners were shuttled from Independence to Richmond. At the preliminary hearing before Judge King in Richmond, Hinkle and several other Mormons who were part of the truce committee testified for the state, after which the elders were charged with "overt acts of treason in Daviess County." Perhaps the most serious charge against Joseph came from Avard, who claimed that the Prophet was "the prime mover and organizer" of the Danites. His evidence made possible the charge of treason. Joseph later wrote that he had been led into the enemy's camp "as a lamb prepared for slaughter," just like the Savior.

Understanding the intentions of the governor and determined to carry them out, General Lucas obtained death warrants from a hastily assembled court-martial and then ordered that the prisoners be shot in the public square in Far West the following morning. But General Alexander Doniphan, charged with carrying out the execution, refused to obey the order. "It is cold-blooded murder," he protested. "I will not obey your order. My brigade shall march for Liberty tomorrow morning, at eight o'clock, and if you execute these men, I will hold you responsible before an earthly tribunal, so help me God."

That threat gave Lucas pause, and the prisoners were safely hustled away to the small town of Liberty. For five months the Prophet and the others languished in the Liberty jail. Joseph used his time preparing statements, mainly intended for the faithful, denying the charges leveled against him. "And now beloved Brethren," he wrote, "we say unto [you] that in as much as God hath said he would have a tried people, that he would purge them as gold now we think that this time he has chosen his own crucible wherein we have been tryed."

With their Prophet in jail, with the militia killing, burning, and looting, and with the governor intent on their extermination or expulsion from the state, the Saints had no other recourse but to flee Missouri. Fortunately they had the leadership of Brigham Young, a senior member of the Quorum of Twelve Apostles, and other elders who kept the brethren together and successfully led them to Illinois and safety. But they left behind most of their belongings, including furniture and clothing, to say nothing of tilled farmland, most of which was instantly seized by greedy scavengers and land jobbers.

The trek toward Illinois by the faithful proved an agony. "I saw one hundred and ninety women and children driven thirty miles across the prairies," reported Lyman Wight. Their lacerated feet bloodied the thinly crusted ice that overlay the ground. Among the refugees was Emma with her four children, the fourth, Alexander, having been born on June 2, 1838. Beneath her skirt she carried two bundles of Joseph's manuscripts of the revisions of the Bible. "I left our house and home," she wrote her husband, "and almost all of everything that we possessed excepting our little children and took my journey out of the State of Missouri, leaving you shut up in that lonesome prison."

It was indeed a trying ordeal for the Prophet. Lacking bedding, decent food, or warmth in his dank, dismal prison cell and unable to stand up straight because of the low ceiling, Joseph cried out, "O God, where art thou? And where is the pavilion that covereth thy hiding place? How long shall thy hand be stayed?" In a revelation God comforted him: "My son, peace be unto thy soul; thine adversity and thine afflictions shall be but a small moment; and then if thou endure it well, God shall exalt thee on high; thou shalt triumph over all thy foes."

At the trial in Liberty on April 6, 1839, Joseph's lawyers again demanded a change of venue, arguing that the prisoners could not be legitimately tried in Daviess County. After several false starts, the change was finally granted from Daviess to Boone County and a "mittimus," or warrant committing a person to jail, was issued, but without citing a name, date, or place. The five prisoners were then herded into two horse-drawn wagons and guarded by four men plus the sheriff. They traveled for two days and then stopped to rest. The prisoners brought along a jug of whiskey with which they treated the entire group. After a few drinks the sheriff showed the prisoners the mittimus and told them that the judge instructed him "never to carry us to Boone county, and never to show the mittimus." A few more drinks and the sheriff announced that he was going to bed. He turned to the prisoners and said suggestively, "You may do as you have a mind to." Three other guards had imbibed freely and also headed off for bed. The fourth actually helped the prisoners saddle the horses. Then two of the prisoners mounted the animals and the other three walked behind. Their change of venue, they decided, would be to Illinois.

Why had they been allowed to escape? Possibly because they were an embarrassment to all concerned. It was enough to drive the Mormons from Missouri. Killing their leaders might win them sympathy from other Americans around the country.

It took ten grueling days for the escapees to reach Quincy,

Illinois, where Young and the other elders had led the rest of the Mormon party. On April 22, 1839, Joseph and company were reunited with their families and found them in reasonably good health. About fourteen thousand brethren had fled Missouri, but they left behind, said Hyrum Smith, scores of men, women, and children murdered "in cold blood, and in the most horrid and cruel manner possible."

Within a few years Far West became a ghost town. No trace of the Mormon settlement remained.

The Saints were treated decently by the citizens of Quincy, but they knew they needed to find a place where they would be relatively secure and separated from hostile Gentiles. A committee was formed to decide on a location, but once the Prophet arrived he considered all the possible locations available to them and determined on a place called Commerce in Hancock County, Illinois. Joseph then turned to the Lord and asked, "What will you have me to do." And the Lord responded, "Build up a city and call my saints to this place."

Chapter 8

Nauvoo

"THIS PLACE" sat on a horseshoe bend of the Mississippi River, about 190 miles north of St. Louis. It is halfway down the state of Illinois and 53 miles north of Quincy. A generally unattractive area, swampy and disease-ridden, it had been the site of an old village of the Sac and Fox tribe of Indians before their removal into unorganized territory in the west. It was called Commerce and had one stone house and three frame and two block houses. For a distance of a mile the ground rose gradually from a low swamp around the river to a bluff that leveled and broadened into prairie lands stretching to the horizon. The place was isolated, in a veritable wilderness thick with trees and underbrush, which made it perfect for these persecuted Mormons in search of rest. But the lower terrain was so wet and impassable that it was deemed unsuitable for permanent settlement. Nevertheless the Prophet believed the swamp could be drained and converted into an attractive area on which to build homes.

Joseph arrived in this wilderness on May 10, 1839, and purchased several plots for the Church from speculators willing to sell on contract. He and his family took up residence on property bought from Hugh and William White for five thousand dollars and investment parcels from Isaac Galland and Horace Hotchkiss for nine thousand dollars—a total of 660 acres. The Smiths lived in a small log cabin on the bank of the river about a mile south of Commerce. And to this desolation the Prophet summoned the faithful. They must be gathered together, he said, so that they could better serve the Lord and live holy and purposeful lives. He laid out the area in lots and sold them to the incoming Saints, reserving the bluff for the temple site. And he changed the name of the town from Commerce to Nauvoo, which he said was a Hebrew word that meant "a beautiful situation, or place, carrying with it, also, the idea of rest." The change became official when the post office adopted it on April 21, 1840.

Lord knows, the Mormons needed a place of rest, away from those who would kill and rob them. They had been harried from state to state, suffering physical and mental torment. But they believed they were called by God through revelation to a higher destiny, and so they responded to Joseph's call. "We had come afoot a thousand miles," remembered one woman. "We lay in bushes, and in barns and outdoors, and traveled until there was a frost just like a snow, and we had to walk on that snow." The Reverend George Peck, a Protestant minister, recorded their arrival. He said he saw "multitudes of people, men, women and children, ragged, dirty, and miserable generally . . . living in tents and covered wagons for lack of better shelter. This strange scene presented itself along the shore for a mile or more. We were informed that they were Mormons who had recently fled from Missouri."

But the Mormons paid a heavy price by living in this swampland. Conditions were so wretched that many of them fell ill from exposure, hunger, and disease. Joseph himself succumbed to illness, but he dragged himself from his sickbed and walked along the riverbank healing the afflicted. His healing powers were reported by several Saints who swore they were witnesses to these miraculous events. Among many others Joseph cured Brigham Young. Mormons likened the Prophet's actions to those of the Savior described in the Gospels, especially his healing of Elijah Fordham, a man said to be dying.

The Prophet approached the bedridden man, took hold of his right hand, and looked deep into Fordham's staring, sightless eyes. Minutes passed. No one spoke. Suddenly a change came over Fordham. His appearance brightened, color returned to his face, and his sight returned. Joseph asked if he recognized him. "Yes," Fordham responded in a whisper.

"Do you believe in Jesus Christ?" Joseph asked.

"I do," came the feeble response.

Whereupon Joseph stood erect, still holding the man's hand, and thundered, "Brother Fordham, I command you in the name of Jesus Christ to arise from this bed and be made whole." The voice was like no other, said one witness, certainly not that of a human being. It sounded like "the voice of God." The house, reported the witness, seemed to shake as though struck by an earthquake. But at Joseph's command Fordham rose from his bed, dressed himself, ate a bowl of bread and milk, and followed the Prophet into the street. Word of this apparent miracle spread quickly among the faithful, reassuring them of their leader's divine calling.

Still the Prophet could not save all. Many died from the swamp fever, including members of his own family. On September 14, 1840, his father succumbed after a long illness, followed on August 7, 1841, by the Prophet's youngest brother, Don Carlos, and then by Joseph's newest son, also named Don Carlos after the infant's uncle.

Racked by disease and hunger, the Saints lived hand to mouth for months on end as they went about the business of building a community and a city. Acting for the Church, Joseph arranged land sales and later became registrar of deeds, a role that made him the controlling hand in any property that was bought or sold in Nauvoo. He fixed the price of city lots at around five hundred dollars but deeded them free to those who had suffered through the Missouri persecution.

One-acre plots were surveyed and sold along the flats of the river. The Saints drained the shoreline and tilled the soil and made it produce. Unlike the Shakers, who built community housing, Mormons erected detached single-family dwellings. Joseph decreed that the city be laid out in four-acre squares like a checkerboard and then cut into one-acre lots with the main square located on the bluff overlooking the Mississippi where the temple would be built. Streets were surveyed and widened to fifty feet, and space was allotted for orchards, kitchens and garden plots, barns, and stables. Over the next several years a number of skilled artisans arrived in Nauvoo, such as blacksmiths, tanners, coopers, potters, and tailors. Soon there were sawmills, gristmills, a printing office, a tannery, a bakery, a gunsmith shop, and a tool factory. There was even "a bonnet maker." Lumber, hacked out of the surrounding forests, and bricks, made locally, provided the basic materials for the building of small dwellings for this burgeoning community.

Because of the ongoing depression created by the Panic of 1837, specie was impossible to obtain. Few Saints had money and so they instituted an exchange system based on letters of credit, IOUs, barter, and bonds provided in land sales. This rather shaky financial system succeeded because of the constant influx of immigrants, who expanded the economy, buttressed by the willingness of the Saints to trust and help one another in their transactions since they were all dedicated to building a great city.

Joseph himself later ran a dry-goods business where he usually met the newcomers who arrived daily and whom he helped get established. These strangers were surprised at how ordinary he looked for a Prophet. He dressed, talked, and acted like any other man, reported one newspaper, and in every respect "appeared exactly the opposite of what" anyone might expect. He was six feet tall and by this time weighed two hundred pounds. He had light brown hair and striking blue eyes. To all he seemed cheerful and gracious, "a man of gentlemanly bearing." One Mormon remarked to his wife, "He is what you ladies would call a very good-looking man." Indeed, the ladies "adored" him. "The love the saints had for him," said one woman, "was inexpressible."

Within a year the population of Nauvoo reached three thousand. Over the next five years, thanks to constantly arriving converts, it grew to fifteen thousand and was the second largest city, after Chicago, in the state. Before long Mormons made up half the population of Hancock County. In a revelation given on January 19, 1841, the brethren living abroad were instructed to gather in the Nauvoo area. As a result hundreds of Mormons flocked to the city from the eastern states and from Canada. They came in canal boats, in covered wagons, and on horseback. Many simply walked.

In early June 1837, while still in Kirtland, Joseph asked his trusted apostle and friend Heber C. Kimball to undertake a mission to England to preach the Gospel and proclaim the Restoration of the Church of Jesus Christ. With that zeal so characteristic of converts, Kimball accepted the invitation and with a small group of associates left for England on June 13. "The idea of being appointed to such an important mission was almost more than I could bear up under," Kimball wrote. "I felt my weakness and was nearly ready to sink under it, but the moment I understood the will of my heavenly Father, I felt a determination to go at all hazards, believing that he would support me by his almighty power." This odyssey marked the introduction of Mormonism in Europe and resulted in between one and two thousand conversions. "Everything we have done has prospered," Kimball happily informed Joseph, "and the God of the Holy Prophets has been with us." When Joseph received this news he rejoiced, "for then I knew that the work of God had taken root in that land."

Now in Nauvoo, the Prophet summoned the Saints in Europe to join the community in Illinois. The Twelve Apostles were sent forth, including Brigham Young, who had barely recovered from his illness, and they soon extended their work from England into France and then Germany, baptizing and bidding all to be gathered to Zion. Starting in 1840 thousands of believers came from Liverpool, England, bringing with them their skills and usually a small amount of money. It was jokingly but truthfully said that immigrants were Nauvoo's biggest import and missionaries its greatest export.

With the expansion of Nauvoo's population the Church purchased property across the river in Iowa and founded a town called Zarahemia and other small settlements in Lee County. Joseph organized a stake in Iowa as he had in Illinois, and elders formed branches wherever Mormons settled. Later the stakes and branches extended throughout North America and Great Britain. Overseeing it all was the Prophet, who through his preaching, revelations, and publications provided dazzling leadership and control of a flock that now numbered in the tens of thousands. He elaborated on Mormon beliefs with thirteen Articles of Faith; he published another revealed scriptural document, the Book of Abraham; he worked with his clerk James Mulholland on the *History of the Church;* and he regularly supervised the distribution of Church periodicals to keep the faithful informed of Church doctrine and membership growth. A newspaper press that had been secretly buried in Far West was dug up and hauled to Nauvoo, where it was re-assembled. In November 1839 the journal *Times and Seasons* came out with its first issue, detailing descriptions of the criminal acts suffered by the Saints in Missouri. Most particularly it was an important source of information and instruction for the entire Mormon community.

The seven-volume *History of the Church of Jesus Christ of Latter-Day Saints,* on which Joseph labored by collecting documentary material, is actually an autobiography and covers less than two decades of the Prophet's life. Prompted by a revelation to provide a record for future generations to study, Joseph began serious work on it in Commerce on June 10, 1839. Originally titled "The History of Joseph Smith," it recounted the Prophet's reputed encounters with the divine. It is written in the first person, although little was dictated or penned by Joseph himself. At least two dozen writers worked on the history, and Thomas Bullock, the Prophet's last secretary, compiled and completed it through March 1, 1843, after Joseph's death. The last year and the death of the founder were set down by George A. Smith, who carried the narrative to the assumption of Brigham Young as head of the Church. These writers fashioned the *History* from diaries, letters, minutes of conferences, sermons, and other documentary material. It was first published from 1852 to 1857 as a series of periodicals. Although it is highly propagandistic, Mormons regard it as generally reliable, despite the fact that it is a secretary or scribe who has written what appears to come directly from Joseph's mouth or pen.

The rapid development of what became a major city on the Mississippi, along with its burgeoning economic success, inevitably antagonized surrounding communities. Gentiles living in Warsaw to the south and Carthage to the east regarded the Nauvoo religious community as a threat to their livelihood because it could rival their river trade. And the easiest way to strike back was by targeting the Mormon religion. They reviled the sect as a hoax and labeled its leader a blasphemer. They dismissed his reported miracles as frauds perpetrated on poor, innocent, and gullible victims. But Joseph was used to this abuse and simply shrugged it off. "The envy and wrath of man have been my common lot all the days of my life," he haughtily remarked.

Joseph had no intention of allowing the persecution the Saints suffered in Missouri to recur in Illinois. If the jealousy and disdain by neighboring townsfolk were the beginning of renewed oppression, he fully intended to bring it to an immediate halt. He made it a point of informing the country via newspapers, personal correspondence, and missionaries of the abominable treatment accorded American citizens in Missouri on account of their religious convictions, and of their brutal massacre at Haun's Mill. He would not let anyone forget Boggs's order to exterminate Mormons and he wanted the nation at large so informed. He demanded redress—in cash, no less—for the losses the Saints had sustained in Missouri. So, on October 29, 1839, he left Nauvoo for Washington to meet with President Van Buren and present to him the grievances of his people and obtain appropriate compensation.

Of course the president was sympathetic when the two men met on November 29, but he was powerless to do anything. "What can I do? I can do nothing," he said. "If I do anything, I shall come in contact with the whole state of Missouri." Even though the Saints had been denied their constitutional rights as citizens of the United States, the president regarded the complaint as a local matter. As for providing money as compensation, only Congress could authorize it, and the likelihood of any such legislation from that body during the ongoing depression was as likely as the outlawing of slavery in the south.

While in Washington Joseph preached before a large crowd, including members of Congress and foreign dignitaries who had heard about him and his new religion. One reporter who was present, Mathew L. Davis, commented on the Prophet's appearance and performance. "He is sincere," Davis wrote. "There is no levity, no fanaticism, no want of dignity in his deportment. He is . . . a very good looking man. . . . He is by profession a farmer, but is evidently well read." He performed no miracles and did not pretend to possess that power. He said that *The Book of Mormon* was communicated to him "*directly from heaven* . . . that he penned it as dictated by God." Toward the end of the sermon Smith admitted that some accused him of "pretending to be a Savior, a worker of miracles, etc. All this is false. . . . He is but a man, he said; a plain, untutored man; seeking what he should do to be saved."

His mission of broadcasting the plight of his Church accomplished, the Prophet returned home in early March 1840 after first visiting with branches of the Church in Pennsylvania and New Jersey.

By this time Joseph undoubtedly experienced a heightened sense of his importance and standing around the country. Here he was tending his flock scattered in different parts of the world, meeting with the president of the United States, and now receiving national attention in the newspapers for what he had created in just a few short years. In a true sense he was an empire builder. Although there were apostates who denounced him, along with Gentiles who feared him, Joseph provided a leadership that was unquestioned. His control of the religious, economic, and political affairs of his community was absolute.

That authority increased quite dramatically when he set to work to fashion a charter for the incorporation of Nauvoo in which all executive, legislative, and judicial powers would ultimately be placed in his hands. Joseph wrote out a frame of government and had it submitted to the Illinois legislature for passage. With political influence exerted by some recent converts, most notably John Cook Bennett, the Illinois General Assembly granted corporate city status to Nauvoo on December 16, 1840. But Joseph boasted, "The City Charter of Nauvoo is of my own plan and device. I concocted it for the salvation of the Church, and on principles so broad that every honest man might dwell secure under its protective influence without distinction of sect or party."

The charter provided for a city council chosen by the electorate and made up of the mayor, four aldermen, and nine councilmen, who were empowered to pass ordinances not in conflict with the state and federal constitutions. This council also had judicial powers, with the mayor serving as chief justice. In addition, the charter permitted the founding of a university. More important, it granted the city the authority to create a militia. Called the Nauvoo Legion when formed, this armed force was composed of two cohorts, mounted and unmounted, each of which was commanded by a brigadier general. Joseph headed this army and was commissioned lieutenant general, an extraordinary rank since no other military officer of the United States held a rank higher than major general. At its peak this army numbered five thousand men and included Mormons and non-Mormons. It constituted the largest armed force in Illinois.

Delighted with his rank, Joseph immediately outfitted himself with a resplendent costume modeled after the U.S. army dress uniform. He wore a blue coat with gold epaulettes, a hat crowned with ostrich feathers, boots reaching up to his knees, and a handsome sword. In this regalia, Joseph sat for a portrait in 1842 by Sutcliffe Maudsley, the only portrait ever done of him while living. It may seem contradictory that a spiritual leader would delight in wearing a gaudy military uniform, but this is another example of Joseph's striking human qualities, qualities that endeared him to his people. As his many disciples repeatedly insisted, Joseph did not act or behave as one might expect of a prophet of God. He seemed as ordinary as any American. He rather enjoyed simple pleasures, they claimed, "just like most folks."

There is no question that Joseph fully intended to use this army to protect his Church. In the past the Saints had been persecuted and driven from state to state. Now they had an army, and Joseph prepared to use it if necessary. The Legion was at the disposal of the mayor to make certain that laws and ordinances of the city were properly executed and obeyed. And since Joseph was the mayor, following a term by James Cook Bennett, he ran Nauvoo like a benevolent despot.

His political power brought warnings and dire predictions from Gentiles, and the Legion excited the envy, jealousy, and fear of surrounding townships. Indeed, its very presence frightened non-Mormon residents of Nauvoo. They mean to "take the world," warned one man. "And if they cannot do it by preaching they will by the force of arms." In no time tensions mounted to the breaking point between hostile neighbors and the Legion, and Joseph was again in the middle of it. So bodyguards were appointed to prevent his assassination.

Another source of irritation that bedeviled the Church was the revelation the Prophet received on January 19, 1841, commanding the Saints to build a hotel to be called Nauvoo House, that would be "a delightful habitation for man, and a resting-place for the weary traveler, that he may contemplate the glory of Zion." What caught in the craw of some brethren was the further command that "my servant Joseph and his seed after him have place in that house, from generation to generation, forever and ever, saith the Lord." Joseph contributed land for the hotel and Church members were called upon by name to invest in the project. Stock certificates were issued and construction began in the spring of 1841. The L-shaped building rose three stories high and ran forty feet deep. The work of finishing the hotel continued for the next three years but was halted in 1846 when the Saints departed Nauvoo after Joseph's assassination. The unfinished structure became the property of Emma Smith, whose second husband, Lewis C. Bidamon, redesigned it into a smaller house where Emma lived until she died on April 30, 1879.

But a more important and immediate reason for the mounting hostility against Joseph and his brethren came with shocking rumors of plural marriages, more popularly known as polygamy. The revelation about plural marriage was dictated by the Prophet on July 12, 1843, a year before his death; it was not publicly announced until August 29, 1852, in Utah, although it had been generally known for some time. Today many Mormon scholars feel there is strong evidence that an unwritten revelation concerning plural marriage came as early as 1831 and that Joseph had married Fanny Alger, although Louisa Beaman, to whom he was sealed on April 5, 1841, is officially regarded as his first plural wife. In fact Joseph wed a number of women, most of them daughters or sisters of leaders of the Church who had been informed of this new doctrine.

It seems that in his study of the Bible in the early 1830s, Joseph queried the Lord about the patriarchs and prophets of the Old Testament who practiced polygamy without committing the sin of adultery. In the recorded revelation of 1843 the Lord responded, "I, the Lord, justified my servants Abraham, Isaac, and Jacob, as also Moses, David and Solomon, my servants, as touching the principle and doctrine of their having many wives and concubines." They did not commit adultery because they acted on the Lord's command. "Therefore, prepare thy heart to receive and obey the instructions which I am about to give you; for all those who have this law revealed unto them must obey the same." The revelation went on at length to explain the terms and conditions of the new covenant—the doctrine of eternal (or sealed) marriage—and it also gave to Joseph the "power to bind and seal on earth and in heaven." The revelation as written then stated that "if any man espouse a virgin and desire to espouse another, and the first give her consent, and if he espouse the second, and they are virgins, and have vowed to no other man, then he is justified and cannot commit adultery." It went on to declare that "if he have ten virgins given unto him by this law, he cannot commit adultery, for they belong to him, and they are given unto him; therefore he is justified."

The revelation recognized that this covenant might be difficult for Emma Smith to accept, and so she was admonished to heed the law. "Let my handmaid, Emma Smith, receive all those that have been given unto my servant Joseph, and who are virtuous and pure before me." Those who are not pure "shall be destroyed, saith the Lord God. For I am the Lord thy God, and ye shall obey my voice."

Although Emma believed in Joseph's prophetic calling and in the divine origin of this new revelation, she had difficulty reconciling herself to the practice, one day agreeing to allow Joseph to be sealed to another woman, the next day adamantly opposed to it. Surprisingly, it was Hyrum, not Joseph, who informed her of this revelation. Mormons believe that Joseph himself initially felt the doctrine repugnant and struggled against it. If in fact it had been revealed to him a decade earlier, he probably withheld its promulgation from the Church because of his struggle with it and his concern about its impact on his followers. But now God had become insistent and wished him to set the example and establish the doctrine even though it might cause disruption in the Church. Friends and confidants of Joseph later stated that only after an angel declared that he must obey this covenant or his calling would be withdrawn and given to another did he finally dictate the revelation and announce it to several of the faithful in Nauvoo. "The object with me," Joseph said, "is to obey & teach others to obey God in just what he tells us to do. It mattereth not whether the principle is popular or unpopular. I will always maintain a true principle even if I Stand alone on it." To Brigham Young, after his return from his mission in England, the Prophet declared that he knew he was risking his life in announcing plural marriage but God had given the commandment and he must obey. Young himself apparently felt a revulsion over the doctrine and said he "could hardly get over it for a long time," that "it was the first time in my life that I desired the grave." He later overcame his revulsion and acquired twenty wives, sixteen of whom bore him fifty-seven children.

Joseph took a number of wives under this new covenant, although the exact figure is still debated; but it is "at least twenty-seven," according to one Mormon historian. Other historians have guessed that it might be as low as a few or as high as eighty-four, many of which were simply sacred sealings for eternity. Most of these marriages occurred in 1842 and

1843. To what extent, if at all, Joseph was influenced by the "free love" doctrines of other religions and communitarian groups at the time, or by the Swedenborgian notion of spiritual marriage for eternity, cannot be determined—but he certainly had access to them and undoubtedly knew of them. Many of his wives were teenagers, the youngest fourteen. There is no certain proof that any of these plural marriages resulted in offspring. However, there is some evidence that Josephine, the child of Emily Dow Partridge, may have been sired by Joseph. Of course there could have been others as well, raised by friends under other names. Six or more of these wives lived with him at one time or another, and it was said that he tried to persuade Nancy Rigdon, the nineteen-year-old daughter of Sidney Rigdon, to marry him. Apparently unaware of the new covenant, Sidney was profoundly shocked by the revelation, although he never came out in open opposition to it.

On July 27, 1842, Joseph married Sarah Ann Whitney, the seventeen-year-old daughter of his friend Newel K. Whitney, who performed the ceremony after the Prophet's revelation to him that it be done and that he speak certain words in the consecration.

One of Joseph's several wives testified that she did not find it particularly difficult to live in the same house with the other wives. "Instead of a feeling of jealousy," she said, "it was a source of comfort to us. We were as sisters to each other."

Bathsheba Smith, the wife of Joseph's cousin George A. Smith, said that she had "met many times with Brother Joseph and . . . heard the Prophet give instructions concerning plural marriage. He counseled the sisters not to trouble themselves in consequences of [this law]; that all would be right—and the result would be for their glory and exaltation."

Critics, of course, argued that Joseph's enormous sexual

appetite—he had been accused of "improper conduct with women" as early as 1830—and Emma's frequent illnesses on account of the hardships she endured, and her difficulties in childbearing, account for this alleged "revelation." But Mormons accept the doctrine as divinely ordained.

In any event, the revelation disturbed a great many in the Church, as might be expected. And rumors of it raised hostility among Gentiles to a fever pitch. But today Mormons are quick to point out that those relatively few Saints who entered into plural marriages experienced crises of faith that were resolved by a personal religious experience in which they believed taking another wife was what God demanded of them. However, several others, including John C. Bennett, who had been instrumental in obtaining Nauvoo's charter, acted as though the revelation amounted to sexual license. These men argued that just telling women they were spiritually married to them allowed the men to engage in sexual relations. Bennett actually preached this contrary doctrine and was forthwith excommunicated. He later toured the country preaching and writing about the alleged sexual orgies indulged in by Mormons.

Actually the practice of plural marriage was carefully regulated in the Church. A plural marriage could be performed only through the sealing power of those in authority. "It is sealed unto them by the Holy Spirit of promise," the revelation read, "by him who is anointed unto whom I have appointed this power and the keys of this priesthood." Mormons believe that monogamy is the general standard, but at special times, as in the biblical age, and for God's own purposes, plural marriage can be practiced without committing sin. Unauthorized polygamy is adultery.

In time acceptance of polygamy became a test of loyalty to

the Church and to Joseph, and the Prophet urged his friends and other elders to follow his example and live as the Lord had commanded. But only a small percentage ever practiced plural marriage in Illinois or later in Utah. The practice was officially ended in 1890, although it continues today in some parts of Utah and elsewhere.

Here was one instance where Joseph boldly departed from his American roots by enunciating a doctrine that sharply conflicted with this nation's commitment to monogamy. Not surprisingly, therefore, the doctrine caused many to abandon the Church; some, like Bennett, felt obliged to publicly revile the faith and denounce Joseph as a sex-mad charlatan.

Joseph faced the storm and kept repeating that he must obey the Lord, that he could do no other. Still he was defying the accepted moral code of the age and breaking secular law. And although he realized that he was inviting trouble and maybe a martyr's death, he persevered in what he believed was the Lord's bidding. He shut his ears to the complaints and kept at his tasks of running the Church, writing its history, and overseeing the completion of the temple in Nauvoo.

Years before, in Kirtland, Joseph had been instructed in a revelation to build a temple in order that God could "endow those whom I have chosen with power from on high." That same command now applied to Nauvoo.

And the construction of a temple was most important because only in this sanctified building could Mormons receive their endowments, a set of ceremonial instructions about the purpose of life. Not until 1842 did Joseph teach that the reception of endowments was necessary to complete the work of the Church, as well as to "prepare the disciples for their missions in the world" and keep them from "being overcome by evils." The ceremony he instituted involved washings and anointings, along with secret grips, the wearing of temple robes, the bestowal of secret names, and other rituals that in some respects resemble Masonic practices. Joseph joined the Masonic order at this time, perhaps because of the economic advantages to be gained by associating with wealthy members of this fraternity, and it may have influenced him in initiating this rite and the way it was celebrated.

In accepting the endowments, an individual promises, among other things, to observe obedience to God, fidelity in marriage, and complete consecration to God's service. Those who have received the endowments may then participate as proxies or agents in the endowment ceremony on behalf of deceased members of their family, so that they may all enter Christ's kingdom and together enjoy eternal life. This is the reason genealogy is so important to Mormons. Today recipients of the endowments obtain sacred underwear, which they must wear at all times except when involved in sports. Temples, which may not be entered by non-Mormons once they are consecrated, are used almost exclusively for the conferring of endowments and the sealing of marriages in eternity. Joseph taught that husbands, wives, and children can be sealed in a binding covenant forever.

The construction of the Nauvoo temple began in the fall of 1840. Designed by William Weeks under Joseph's close supervision, the structure with its tower and spire had to conform to what the Prophet had seen in a vision. It was built at the top of a sloping hill overlooking the Mississippi River and measured 128 feet long and 88 feet wide. The top of the tower rose 158 feet above the ground and was crowned with a golden statue of an angel flying in a horizontal position. Unlike many

Christian churches, Mormon temples do not have a cross at the top of the spire.

The lower level of the building had a baptismal font for the baptism for the dead, whereby living Mormons can act as proxies for their deceased ancestors and others. Joseph taught this doctrine in a funeral sermon he gave in August 1840 for Seymour Brunson; it allows the deceased recipient, exercising freedom of choice, to accept Christ and enter His Kingdom. Those who choose to reject Christ are not so rewarded.

The first floor of the temple was a large center room that served as an auditorium; the second floor was shaped like the first; and the attic above contained two main sections: the west end, used for endowment ordinances, and the east end, for sealing eternal marriages. The stone for the building was quarried near the city, but the wood was floated down the Mississippi River on rafts from Wisconsin to Nauvoo.

The cost of the structure exceeded one million dollars, much of it covered by tithes and gift offerings of the Saints, who were called upon to make sacrifices as commanded by the Lord. Most gave their talent and time, working months on end from sunup to sundown, even in inclement weather. On May 1, 1846, two years after Joseph's death, the temple was dedicated in a three-day service witnessed by thousands, including visitors who paid one dollar for the privilege of attending. The dedication came at approximately the same time that the main body of Saints deserted Nauvoo and followed Brigham Young across the plains into the Rocky Mountains to escape new and even more intense persecution by their enemies. Some Mormons remained, including Emma, only to witness the destruction of the temple when it was deliberately set ablaze in October 1848 and later suffered the devastating effects of a tornado that knocked down its walls.

But much of the beauty of Nauvoo as built by the Mormons remains to this day; the city is virtually a museum. Brigham Young later called Nauvoo the "City of Joseph." It was everything the Prophet had worked for and planned. He really made it a "beautiful place."

Chapter 9

Assassination

BECAUSE OF THE CONTINUING economic depression around the country, the Democratic party—the party of Andrew Jackson—was trounced in the presidential election of 1840 by the opposing Whig party of John Quincy Adams, Henry Clay, and Daniel Webster. Jackson's handpicked successor, Martin Van Buren, was defeated for reelection by the Whig candidate, General William Henry Harrison, whose only personal credential for the office, as far as most people were concerned, was his victory over the Indians at Tippecanoe Creek in Indiana in 1811. In one of the most roaring, rollicking political campaigns in American history—"Tippecanoe and Tyler, Too, Van, Van is a used up man"—Americans unceremoniously dumped the Democrats and turned the government over to the Whigs. They expected Harrison in the White House, Henry Clay in the Senate, and their majority party in Congress to restore the country to prosperity and renewed economic growth. Unfortunately Harrison died one month after taking office and his running mate and successor, John Tyler, turned out to be a Democrat in disguise. Earlier he had bolted Jackson's party over the nullification issue, but his economic principles and ideas of government remained solidly Democratic. He vetoed the most important legislation proposed by the Whig leadership, especially a bill to charter another national bank, and he was promptly read out of the party. Nevertheless, during his four years in office, the nation slowly emerged from its economic slump and began the process of recovery.

Nauvoo also prospered during the Tyler administration, but it was run strictly according to Mormon beliefs. There were no saloons in the town, and when "devils" dared to open a brothel it was immediately closed and the building torn down. Quite simply, Nauvoo was a theocracy controlled by a single individual in concert with a council.

In February 1841 the governor of the state, Thomas Carlin, approved the incorporation of the Nauvoo Agricultural and Manufacturing Association with capital stock of $100,000— much to the consternation of rival river towns and nearby communities with less successful entrepreneurs. This development added to a steadily increasing wariness and jealousy among the town's neighbors; and when Joseph paraded in his brilliantly decorated uniform with its ostrich feathers and shining sword and drilled some two thousand men organized into cavalry and infantry, the wariness turned to alarm. These men had rifles, not muskets like the state militia, and the possibility that this fighting force could be turned against non-Mormons sent Gentiles into angry fits of protest. It did not help that Joseph boasted that if the Saints were molested in any way he would establish their God-given rights with the sword. Nor did it help when he petitioned Congress for authorization to raise an even larger army if necessary to protect his people. Joseph could be brutal; he was a hardheaded pragmatist who fully appreciated the power and authority he now possessed. In no way would he turn the other cheek in his determination to protect the Saints from harm. "Beware, oh earth! how you fight against the Saints of God and shed innocent blood," he wrote, for "in the days of Elijah, his enemies came upon him, and fire was called down from heaven to destroy them."

On April 6, 1841, the Mormon Church demonstrated its full strength and splendor. To commemorate the eleventh anniversary of the founding of the Church and to celebrate the laying of the temple's cornerstone, the Nauvoo Legion paraded through the town to the cheers and shouts of the faithful. Fourteen companies of the Legion, together with two companies of volunteers from Ohio, many dressed in glittering uniforms, saluted their lieutenant general. They marched smartly toward the temple grounds with the Prophet following behind. A military band accompanied them, and artillery and cannon fire added to the tumult. A handmade silk American flag was presented to the general by the ladies of Nauvoo and he proudly displayed it as he rode triumphantly through the streets.

At noon a large crowd of people gathered before the temple site. Joseph, the architect who designed the building, and other guests took their places on the stand, and the ceremonies began with hymns, prayers, and choir singing. Then Sidney Rigdon, the acclaimed orator, gave the principal address, after which the cornerstone was laid. It was an impressive scene and visibly demonstrated what Nauvoo and the Mormon Church had accomplished in just a few short years.

By the early 1840s Joseph Smith had a national and international reputation, thanks to the tens of thousands who belonged to his Church in America and Europe. In addition he was Nauvoo's mayor, chief justice, lieutenant general, trustee of the university, real estate agent, publisher of a monthly newspaper, proprietor of a store, part owner of a Mississippi steamboat, a subscriber to the Nauvoo Agricultural and Manufacturing Association, and a member of the newly formed Masonic lodge—in all, a commanding figure within the state of Illinois. Most important, he was the First President of the Church of Jesus Christ of Latter-day Saints, who enjoyed the authority of a "prophet, translator and seer."

Having organized the men of Nauvoo, Joseph next turned to the women. In 1842 he founded the Female Relief Society, whose members were to attend to the needs of the poor and to correct the "morals" and strengthen the "virtues of the female community." They were to "provoke the brethren to good works" and seek "after objects of charity." He appointed his first wife, Emma, as president of the society. Joseph seemed to want it understood that despite his many other wives, he remained devoted to Emma and protective of her. Said one Mormon: "Although at the time he had in the Mansion [the home Joseph built and moved into in 1842] other wives, younger and apparently more brilliant, yet Emma, the wife of his youth, to me, appeared the queen of his heart and of his home."

James Gordon Bennett, the distinguished journalist, took note of the Prophet in an editorial of November 18, 1841, in his newspaper, the *New York Herald*. "There can be no mistake in Joseph Smith. He is a master spirit—and his ambition is to found a religious empire that will reach the uttermost ends of the earth. He has given the world a new Bible—and he is now busily engaged in founding a new kingdom of the faithful." In subsequent numbers of his newspaper Bennett reported how "the Holy City of God, Nauvoo," had risen to a major metropolis and he compared the religious observances and military organization of Joseph to those of Muhammad and Islam.

Joseph rather liked some of the things Bennett had said of

him and reprinted those parts in the Mormon newspaper, *Times and Seasons.* But other newspapers carried very different accounts of the Mormon Church and its leader. Joseph's plural marriages naturally outraged many Americans, and his political power brought warnings and dire predictions from non-Mormons. Joseph Smith's "awful claims to divine inspiration," wrote one man in an article published in the Alton, Illinois, *Telegraph* of November 14, 1840, "make his voice to believers like the voice of God." As a consequence they "hold in their hands a fearful balance of political power." With it they can "surround our institutions with an element of danger, more dreaded than an armed and hundred eyed police." Moreover, the size and strength of the Nauvoo Legion was of particular concern. One army officer figured that the Mormon armed force would soon reach fifty thousand and would constitute a genuine threat to the liberty of the country. "The time will come," he warned in a newspaper article, "when this gathering host of religious fanatics will make this country shake to its centre. A western empire is certain!"

Then, when someone attempted to murder the Prophet's former nemesis Lilburn W. Boggs, the governor of Missouri, many immediately suspected and charged "Joe Smith" with instigating the attack. Warrants were issued to extradite Joseph to Missouri to stand trial, and the situation became so personally dangerous to him that he was forced to go into hiding.

Joseph's position was certainly not helped in early 1844 when the apostles decided that none of the candidates in the approaching presidential election were worthy of support and accordingly nominated the Prophet as their candidate for president, with Rigdon as vice president. In the new nationalistic spirit of "Manifest Destiny" that was sweeping the country, the

Democratic party had rejected the candidacy of both Tyler and Van Buren and had nominated James Knox Polk of Tennessee, on a platform calling for the annexation of both Texas (which had won its independence from Mexico eight years earlier) and the Oregon country clear up to the southern boundary (54°40') of Russian Alaska. "54°40' or fight" was the cry.

The doctrine of Manifest Destiny first appeared in an article by John L. O'Sullivan in the *Democratic Review*, which he both founded and edited. In the article he said that it "is by the right of manifest destiny" for the United States "to overspread and to possess the whole of the continent which Providence has given us for the development of the great experiment in liberty and federative self government entrusted to us." This continent belongs to us by divine right, trumpeted spread-eagle nationalists, and we mean to take it and hold it.

The Whig party nominated Henry Clay, who feared that territorial expansion would trigger a war with Mexico over the annexation of Texas or a war with Great Britain, which also claimed the Oregon country. In addition it would excite sectional passions over the mounting opposition to slavery in the north, resulting from the abolitionist crusade of the past twenty and more years.

With candidates like Polk and Clay, the Mormons thought they could do a great deal better with Smith and Rigdon. The platform for their candidates consisted of the abolition of imprisonment for debt; reduction of taxes through a program of strict governmental economy; the petitioning of slave states to abolish slavery; the annexation of Texas, Mexico, and Canada with their consent; and the reestablishment of a national bank with branches in each state. Missionaries—the Church was now turning out hundreds of missionaries to preach the Restored

Gospel—fanned out across northern states to campaign for their ticket.*

It was at this time that Joseph organized the secret Council of Fifty to assist his political ambitions. It was a virtual "shadow government," according to one Mormon historian. That body anointed Joseph "King, Priest and Ruler over Israel on Earth." Some members of the Church worried that his personal goals contradicted what a Prophet should be about, that his ambition now bordered on "corruption and wickedness." They also accused him of profiting from land speculation and lusting after personal wealth.

It was worse among Gentiles in Nauvoo and the surrounding towns. They feared the rapidly expanding political power of this "King, Priest and Ruler." Joseph's "black heart would exult in carnage and bloodshed," wrote Thomas Gregg, an anti-Mormon journalist, "rather than yield one iota of what power he had obtained by his hellish knavery." Later Gregg added, "Your career of infamy cannot continue but a little longer! Your days are numbered!"

The *Warsaw Signal* of May 29, 1844, agreed. "Joe Smith is not safe out of Nauvoo," declared Thomas Sharp, the editor. "We would not be surprised to hear of his death by violent

---

*During the campaign Clay tried to hedge on the question of expansion, and in the fall election of 1844 he was narrowly defeated by Polk. Several months later President Tyler called upon Congress to pass a joint resolution admitting Texas into the Union. The resolution passed and was signed by Tyler on March 1, 1845. Texas ratified annexation on July 4 and was admitted into the Union on December 29, 1845. Polk was inaugurated president on March 4, 1845, and later accepted a treaty worked out with Great Britain on June 15, 1846, that divided the disputed Oregon country between Canada and the United States at the 49th parallel.

means in a short time. He has deadly enemies." Resentment, declared the editorial, is at fever pitch, "and it will break forth in fury upon the slightest provocation."

That provocation came soon enough. Retaliating against recent criticism of his leadership, Joseph ordered the "smashing" of the printing press of an opposition newspaper, the *Nauvoo Expositor*, which had labeled him "one of the blackest and basest scoundrels that has appeared upon the stage of human existence." Worse, it said, he had established a special armed force of forty men to patrol the streets of Nauvoo day and night, setting up a virtual police state. In addition it was known that he had petitioned Congress to give him the authority to summon United States troops to assist him in putting down mob violence against Mormons whenever it occurred.

The destruction of the *Expositor* finally triggered demands from surrounding towns that something be done about the "ruthless, lawless, ruffian band of Mormon mobocrats, at the direction of that unprincipled wretch Joe Smith." We "leave it to the Public," editorialized the *Warsaw Signal*, "to avenge this climax of insult & injury."

Joseph wrote a defense of his actions to the Illinois governor, Thomas Ford, but the rising anger in Carthage continued unabated. He and several others were charged with instigating a riot involved in the destruction of the *Expositor*, and the sheriff was sent to arrest them. A Nauvoo court stepped in, however, and issued a writ under which the accused were tried and subsequently acquitted. When the sheriff returned to Carthage without the prisoners, hundreds of angry citizens assembled and demanded the expulsion of Mormons from the area, whereupon Joseph called out the Nauvoo Legion and placed the city under martial law to prepare for an imminent assault.

"CITIZENS ARISE, ONE AND ALL!!!" screamed the

Warsaw Signal in response on June 12. "Can you stand by, and suffer such infernal devils! to rob men of their property rights, without avenging them. We have no time for comment; every man will make his own. LET IT BE MADE WITH POWDER AND BALL."

At this juncture Governor Ford intervened. On visiting Carthage he found the situation bordering on open warfare. He sent Joseph instructions to come to Carthage to answer the grave charges leveled against him and prove his willingness to abide by the law and placate public outrage.

Fearing for his life if he surrendered, Joseph decided to flee the city and head west. He, his brother Hyrum, and two others crossed the Mississippi and found temporary shelter with one of the brethren. He sent back a letter to Emma telling her that he intended to go to Washington to plead his case before President Tyler. But in her response she begged him to return and surrender to the governor. Nauvoo was in turmoil. Reports of his flight had spread through the town, and fears of another extermination order brought the faithful close to panic. Without the Prophet they did not know what to do or where to turn. Hundreds packed up and left the city, especially merchants. Joseph was accused of cowardice by some for deserting his flock in their hour of peril. Would the Savior have acted in such a despicable manner?

That charge struck home. A good shepherd does not desert. He defends his flock, even if it costs him his life.

Joseph turned to Hyrum. "Brother Hyrum," he said, "you are the oldest, what shall we do?"

"Let us go back and give ourselves up," came the reply.

"We shall be butchered," Joseph protested.

"The Lord is in it. If we live or die, we shall be reconciled to our fate."

Clearly Joseph showed once again a side of human weakness in running away from danger. He rightly feared for his life, and he did not wish to die. He had to be reminded of his station and calling. He had to be reminded to place his trust in the Lord.

This story resonates with a clear echo of Christ in Gethsemane. It is interesting to note that so much of Joseph's life, as reported by Mormon sources, has parallels in the Gospels. Since he believed—he always believed—that he had been chosen by God to restore the true Church, he must have known that, like Christ, he might be expected to sacrifice his life in order to validate his mission. When the moment came for a final decision, he willingly consented to it.

The brothers recrossed the river and returned home. Joseph wrote to the governor that he would surrender to him in Carthage the next day. On Monday, June 24, 1844, at 6:30 in the morning, Joseph, Hyrum, John Taylor, Porter Rockwell, William W. Phelps, and other members of the Nauvoo city council who had been charged with riot in destroying the *Expositor* rode out of Nauvoo and headed for Carthage. Along the way Joseph told several bystanders that he "expected to be murdered. There appeared no alternative but that he must give himself up, or the inhabitants of the city would be massacred by a lawless mob under the sanction of the Governor." He said he felt like a lamb going to the slaughter.

As the Prophet reached Carthage, a company of militiamen approached with an order from the governor that the Nauvoo Legion be disbanded. Joseph countersigned the order and agreed to return to the city to ensure its compliance. Several small cannons and about two hundred firearms were subsequently surrendered, but Joseph advised the brethren to hide all personal guns in a warehouse in case of trouble.

At 6:00 P.M. he and the others in his party and the accompanying militia returned to Carthage, arriving at midnight. A jeering, angry mob greeted them. "God damn you, old Joe, we've got you now," they reportedly shouted. "He has seen the last of Nauvoo. Stand away, you [militia] boys, and let us shoot the damned Mormons. Kill all the damn Mormons."

Joseph and his followers were hauled away to Hamilton's Hotel and Tavern, where they were to be temporarily incarcerated. It was also the place where Governor Ford was staying. Once the prisoners were safely locked up, Ford persuaded the mob to disperse.

The next day the prisoners had a preliminary hearing before Robert F. Smith, a justice of the peace and the captain of the Carthage Greys, a notoriously anti-Mormon contingent of the militia. They were charged with riot. Released on bond of seventy-five hundred dollars and ordered to appear for trial at the next term of the circuit court, most of the accused left for Nauvoo—except Joseph and Hyrum. They returned to the hotel to speak with the governor.

At eight o'clock that night a constable appeared with a mittimus signed by Robert F. Smith demanding that Joseph and Hyrum be held in jail until tried for treason. They protested that the mittimus was illegal because it had not been introduced at the hearing. They appealed to Governor Ford, but he refused to intervene, stating that he had no authority to keep an officer of the court from performing his duty. Accordingly the two men, with eight of their friends attending them—including Willard Richards, Dan Jones, Stephen Markham, and John Taylor—were carted off to jail to the accompanying taunts of a rabble that had gathered in the streets and around the hotel. Markham and Jones walked on either side of the Prophet to protect him from harm, but several times the mob broke through the ranks of the guards before being shoved back.

It was probably a wise move to get them out of the hotel to what everyone thought would be a place of safety. The jailhouse was a small two-story building of stone surrounded by a low fence. The first floor provided quarters for the jailer and his family. A stairway led to the second floor, which was divided into a debtors' room and a small cell that had only mattresses on the floor.

The jailer, George W. Stigall, and his wife received the prisoners and directed them to the debtors' room. This room had two windows, a large fireplace, a double bed, and some chairs. There were no bars on the windows nor lock on the door. Hardly a secure room. Joseph's friends were permitted to stay with the prisoners for the night, and most of them slept on the floor.

The next day Joseph requested a meeting with the governor. But the interview accomplished nothing except that Ford agreed to take the two men with him if he decided to visit Nauvoo, since it was Joseph's unshakable belief that he would be assassinated if the governor left Carthage.

That night five of their friends, including Richards, Taylor, and Jones, remained with the prisoners. They prayed and read *The Book of Mormon* before falling asleep. Several hours later a gunshot near the jail awakened Joseph. He left the bed and whispered to Jones, "Are you afraid to die?"

"Has that time come, think you?" the frightened man replied. But Joseph reassured him that all would be well.

The next morning, June 27, 1844, at Joseph's bidding, Jones went to find out the cause of the overnight disturbance. To his horror he heard repeatedly that as soon as the governor and the militia had left town a mob would kill the Prophet and his brother "if we have to tear the jail down" in the process.

Jones rushed to the governor to report what he had heard, but Ford assured him that he was unnecessarily alarmed. "The people are not that cruel," he insisted. Later that morning he left town for Nauvoo, declaring that he had changed his mind about taking Joseph and Hyrum with him because it would be dangerous and might cause a riot that would involve innocent women and children. He then ordered the militia at Carthage and Warsaw to disband, except for the troops to go with him to Nauvoo and the Carthage Greys to remain behind to guard and protect the prisoners. Could this have been a setup for assassination? Mormons think so, but there is no clear evidence that Ford's decision was anything more than a stupid mistake.

Back at the jail the thirty-eight-year-old Joseph dictated a letter to Emma and added a postscript in his own hand. "Dear Emma, I am very much resigned to my lot, knowing I am justified, and have done the best that could be done. Give my love to the children and all my friends." Shortly thereafter the remainder of Joseph's friends, except for Richards and Taylor, were ordered to leave the jail. One of the brethren, John S. Fullmer, slipped a single-barreled pistol into Joseph's pocket while another, Cyrus H. Wheelock, smuggled a fully loaded six-shooter into the jail under his raincoat. The Prophet handed the single-barreled pistol to Hyrum, who protested. "I hate to use such things or see them used," he said.

"So do I," Joseph replied. "But we may have to defend ourselves."

Regretfully, Hyrum took the pistol.

The four men just sat and sweated in the mounting heat and humidity. Taylor, who had a pleasant voice, was asked to sing a popular hymn, "A Poor Wayfaring Man of Grief," about a suffering individual who turns out to be Jesus.

About 5:00 P.M. Jailer Stigall suggested that the prisoners move to the cell, where they would be safer. Joseph agreed to go after supper. Meanwhile a mob gathered, their faces painted dark brown, and headed for the jail. They jumped the fence, circled the jail, and broke open the door. There was a scuffle and a shout to surrender, followed by three or four shots.

Willard Richards ran to the window and saw that the building was surrounded. He gave an alarm, whereupon Joseph grabbed the six-shooter and Hyrum the pistol. Richards and Taylor threw themselves against the door. More shots were fired. Swearing, shouting, and shooting, the mob charged up the stairway and threw their weight against the door. A shower of bullets blasted through the door. One of them struck Hyrum in the face.

"I am a dead man," he moaned, as a second, third, and fourth bullet struck him. He slumped to the floor.

Joseph leaned over him. "Oh, my dear brother Hyrum!" he cried. And with that he jumped up, pried open the door a few inches and fired his six-shooter into the passageway. Two or three times the gun misfired, although it was claimed that he wounded three or four men. Then he thrust his fist through the open door and punched a man in the neck.

No longer able to hold back the mob, John Taylor ran to the window with the intention of jumping to the ground. A shot from the passageway brought him down and struck his watch, which probably saved his life. His watch stopped at sixteen minutes and twenty-six seconds past five o'clock. He collapsed on the floor as several more bullets pierced his body, "splattering his blood like rain upon the walls and floor."

His gun empty, Joseph dropped it to the floor. His friends urged him to escape through the window. He sprang to the sill and as he did so two shots from the door struck him. At the same time another ball hit him through the window from a distance of fifty or sixty yards, shot by someone standing outside, probably a Carthage Grey. It pierced his right breast. He pitched forward and let out a cry, "O Lord, my God!" and fell out of the window to the ground below.

He rolled on his face. One of the mob seized the body and propped it up on one side of the well curb, as though positioning Joseph for execution. Colonel Levi Williams ordered four men to shoot the Prophet. Standing eight feet away, they fired simultaneously and once again Joseph fell forward on his face.

At that point someone screamed, "The Mormons are coming," whereupon the mob hastily exited the jail and headed for the woods, thus sparing the lives of Richards and Taylor, who later recovered from their ordeal and duly reported what had happened. Joseph's body was placed alongside that of his brother. A wagon carried the remains of the two men to the hotel until coffins could be made. On Friday morning, June 28, Richards drove the bodies back to Nauvoo, where ten thousand people assembled to hear Richards and Markham beg them to keep the peace and leave the punishment of the murderers to God.

Of the sixty-odd men suspected of murdering Joseph and Hyrum Smith, nine were later indicted, but none was ever found guilty. Justice was denied the Prophet and his brother.

The bodies were taken to Mansion House and the coffins covered with black velvet. The coffins were then laid in rough pine boxes. Thousands of mourners filled the house to bid their Prophet a final farewell. On seeing her dead sons, Lucy, as she later remembered, cried out "in the agony of my soul, 'My God, my God, why hast thou forsaken this family!' A voice replied, 'I have taken them to myself, that they might have rest.'" In a state of complete shock and barely conscious, Emma had to be carried back to her room.

Fearing the desecration of the graves, the church leaders decided on a mock funeral. The coffins were lifted from the pine boxes and secured in a bedroom. A bag of sand was placed at each end of the two empty boxes. At night the boxes were carried in a hearse to the graveyard and interred in a regular ceremony. But secretly, at midnight, ten men buried the coffins in the basement of the unfinished Nauvoo House, the foundation of which had been completed. After the burial a thunderstorm raged and the rain washed away all traces of the grave. Months later Emma had Joseph's body moved to a secret location behind a cottage. There it rested in an unmarked grave until 1928, when it was reburied in a new grave in Nauvoo along with the remains of Emma and Joseph's brother: Emma on the left, Joseph in the middle, and Hyrum on the right.

This brutal and unjustified killing raises a question asked again and again: Why were Joseph and his Mormon brethren hated with such intensity as to provoke mob violence and murder? The reasons, of course, are many and reveal much about the Second Great Awakening. To start, there was Joseph's contention that all other religions and their preachers were corrupt and an abomination in the sight of God. Only the Mormon Church was the true Church of Jesus Christ. In this highly charged religious atmosphere, that claim alone antagonized and provoked rival clergymen and their congregations. They felt he demeaned what they held sacred. Then there were the stories of his revelations, about how he dug up and translated gold plates and spoke regularly to God, and how God provided him with new covenants and the keys of the Kingdom. Moreover, Joseph's insistence that he had brought forth another Bible that provided a true history of the lost tribes of Israel appeared to some as outright blasphemy. He also dared to assert that the King James Version of the Bible contained errors and was incomplete, a claim that infuriated members of established churches because that was their Bible, their sacred scripture, their contact with the Godhead. In modern times all these contentions would probably be dismissed by other religious leaders as the ravings of a misguided fanatic. Not so in this Jacksonian age. Not when widespread mob violence was commonplace, especially against Native Americans, African-Americans, and Catholics, to name the most obvious. Americans were a violent people, especially on the frontier, and it did not take much for them to resort to violence when provoked. Joseph uttered explosive words during the course of his ministry and they triggered explosive responses.

To make matters worse, the Mormon religion seemed to make a mockery of fundamental Christian beliefs, with such teachings as polygamy, eternal matter, baptism for the dead, a plurality of gods, men and women becoming gods themselves, God the Father being once a man who passed through a stage of mortality before becoming God, and other such "ludicrous" doctrines. The longer Joseph lived, said some, the more "grotesque" his ideas about God and religion became. All the more reason to get rid of him. To many, Joseph was nothing but a sex-mad fraud who defamed religion and swindled the gullible out of their property.

There were also economic factors behind the bigotry. Either Mormons were criticized when impoverished because they placed an "insupportable burden of pauperism" on the community; or when prosperous they aroused the jealousy and resentment of those less fortunate, who plotted to drive them from the community in order to seize their property.

Furthermore, intolerance toward Mormons frequently sprang from their clannishness. They tended to act together, vote together, and patronize only Mormon establishments—a charge that can still be heard today. They formed a voting bloc that seemed to threaten the freedoms of non-Mormons. For example, in one local election in 1843, Hyrum Smith announced, with Joseph's approval, that he had received a revelation instructing Mormons to vote for the Democratic candidate—which they did. From that moment on, said Governor Ford, partisans of the two major political parties "determined upon driving the Mormons out of the State."

As for Joseph's assassination, it is most probable that he was executed for the simple reason that his political activities had become extremely dangerous to the citizens of surrounding towns. He had built a theocratic dictatorship in Nauvoo guarded by a standing army of five thousand heavily armed men, the largest army in the state, whose very existence terrorized Gentiles. Worse, he attempted to negotiate with the central government for authority to summon an army of one hundred thousand to protect his people wherever they might reside. Then he and the city council dispatched what appeared to some as ambassadors to England, France, and Russia, as though Nauvoo were an independent, sovereign state, separate from the United States. Finally Joseph had the audacity to run for the presidency of the United States during a period of heightened tension over territorial expansion, abolition, and the likelihood of war with Mexico.

His candidacy was the last straw. In the minds of many he had become a menace to freemen everywhere and had to be eliminated. The courts repeatedly failed to rein him in, so a mob took it upon themselves to end his life and the danger he posed. His murder was a political act of assassination.

With Joseph's death the Saints had lost their leader, the very reason for their existence as a Church. Devastated by their loss, they hardly knew where to turn. Several men came forward to claim the succession, but Emma and Joseph's brother William insisted that it should fall to Joseph's eldest son, Joseph III. Since the boy was only twelve it was felt that William should lead the Church until Joseph III came of age.

But the two strongest contenders for the office of First President were Brigham Young and Sidney Rigdon.* Late in March 1844 Joseph had conferred on the Quorum of the Twelve all the ordinances, keys, and authority he possessed. At a conference called to decide the succession, the assembled members agreed to sustain the decision of the Twelve. Since Brigham Young was the president of the Twelve, he took control of Church affairs and in 1846 led some sixteen thousand beleaguered Saints to Utah. The situation in Nauvoo had become so desperate, with further killings and burning of farms and crops, that the governor advised Brigham Young to leave the state.

Five months after Joseph's murder, his and Emma's youngest son, David Hyrum, was born on November 17, 1844. (Emma bore nine children, only four of whom lived to maturity.) She

---

*After Church members rejected his bid for what he called a guardianship, Rigdon attempted to form a rival leadership and was excommunicated. He then organized a Church of Christ in Pennsylvania and later the Church of Jesus Christ of the Children of Zion, which lasted until the 1880s. He died in 1876.

and her children remained behind in Nauvoo, as did the Prophet's mother, Lucy Mack Smith,* and the Reorganized Church of Jesus Christ of Latter-day Saints was forged at a formal conference of Church leaders on June 12–13, 1852. It renounced polygamy and disavowed any connection with the Church in Utah. In 2001 it officially changed its name to the Community of Christ.

But the Saints who took the long, agonizing trek across the plains into the Rocky Mountains with Brigham Young found refuge in a valley next to the Great Salt Lake. Exercising the many virtues that are uniquely Mormon—their industry, resilience, dedication, determination, and commitment to one another and their Church—they made the valley bloom through irrigation and through their constant attention to and application of improved farming equipment and methods. Immigrants poured into the community from eastern states, Canada, and Great Britain. Within a decade their settlements extended over three hundred miles in all directions. Missionaries continued to go forth to preach the Restored Gospel and invite converts to relocate in Zion. By the time Brigham Young died in 1877—he had been sustained as First President of the Church in 1847—some one hundred thousand Mormons lived in the Utah Territory. They founded over two hundred cities, towns, and villages and established numerous schools, factories, and mills. In 1890 the Church terminated plural marriage and six years later, on January 4, 1896, Congress admitted Utah as the forty-fifth state in the Union.

In the twentieth century the Church continued to expand

---

*Lucy died in 1856, three years after the publication of her *Biographical Sketches*.

and prosper. By this time it had won respectability and acceptance from most Americans.

All this began because of the alleged visions and revelations of one man. Joseph Smith Jr. lived a relatively short life, dying at the age of thirty-eight. A charismatic leader and an organizing genius, he founded a Church that in a little over fourteen years numbered between twenty-five and thirty thousand. It has been estimated that since its founding the membership of the Mormon Church has grown by 10 percent each decade—which is truly astounding. By the middle of the twenty-first century that number is expected to exceed fifty million and the Church will rank among the top five Christian denominations in the United States.

As a prophet Joseph was burdened by many human frailties. He craved recognition and appreciation of his work. Shrewd and even cunning at times, he was a proud man who knew his own worth yet suffered many moments of insecurity and self-doubt. At once kind and generous toward others, he also scrambled after material gain for himself and his Church. He had a deeply controlling temperament and brooked no opposition to his leadership. An optimist, he remained steadfast in his beliefs to the end, despite repeated reversals and defeats. In him the strains of egotism, pragmatism, courage, gentleness, pretension, and jealousy were blended together. A man of little formal education but of striking intellectual power, he produced a vast amount of religious writing that has influenced millions of people around the world.

Some historians have questioned whether Joseph really believed he was a prophet. They regard him as a charlatan who took advantage of the gullibility of vulnerable and frightened people. Others suggest he came to believe in his cause only after thousands accepted his claims and joined his Church. Mormons, of course, insist that from the very beginning Joseph Smith Jr. understood that God had chosen him to restore His Church in preparation for the Second Coming. He was obviously a remarkable man who accomplished something truly exceptional. He faltered at times in carrying out his mission, but he held to his course until the very end.

To a large extent Smith and his Church were products of a uniquely American milieu. The Jacksonian age with its democratic thrust and reach for perfection provided the conditions and impetus for sudden and massive changes throughout the country. And while it is true that in the first half of the nineteenth century the Second Great Awakening helped bring about or advance a great many social reforms in the United States (abolition, women's rights, the rise of popular and democratic Christianity, prison reform, temperance, and so on), it also released a certain amount of religious bigotry that, when combined with violence, produced murderous rampages.

And today the Great Awakenings of the past have not been forgotten. They were remembered in a lead editorial of the *New York Times* on January 20, 2001, after President George W. Bush recommended channeling federal funds to "faith-based" groups to serve social needs. "American religion may well be going through a revival that some scholars say is comparable to the 'great awakenings' of the past, but it would surely be dangerous," the newspaper warned, "to link that revival too closely with government involvement." Mixing religion and politics can have disastrous consequences and release forces that tarnish the most cherished ideals of American justice, democracy, and liberty, a fact that needs to be remembered by everyone, whether religious (like Joseph) or not.

During the Second Great Awakening those forces brought about the violent death of a decent man who claimed to be a prophet of God. But they could not extinguish his message or the promise he made to his followers of their ultimate triumph. They could not prevent the Church of Jesus Christ of Latter-day Saints from achieving global recognition and acceptance.

SOURCES

Chapter 1: **The Second Great Awakening**

Most of the quotations in this chapter come from Lucy Smith, *Biographical Sketches of Joseph Smith the Prophet and His Progenitors for Many Generations* (Liverpool, 1853, Plano, Ill., 1880), pp. 22–31, 39, 57–60; Richard L. Bushman, *Joseph Smith and the Beginnings of Mormonism* (Urbana and Chicago, 1984), pp. 22–25; D. Michael Quinn, *Early Mormonism and the Magic World View* (Salt Lake City, 1998), pp. 15–16, 31, 41; Robert V. Remini, *The Jacksonian Era* (Arlington Heights, Ill., 1989), pp. 70–92; *Niles Weekly Register,* February 18, March 4, 1815; and Gordon B. Hinckley, *What of the Mormons* (Salt Lake City, 1954), pp. 12–13. But see also Whitney Cross, *Burned-Over District* (New York, 1950), and Frances Trollope, *Domestic Manners of the Americans* (London, 1832); Alice Felt Tyler, *Freedom's Ferment* (Minneapolis, 1944); William G. McLoughlin, *Revivals, Awakenings, and Reform* (New York, 1978); and Dickson D. Bruce, *And They All Sang Hallelujah: Plain-Folk Camp-Meeting Religion, 1800–1845* (Knoxville, 1974).

Chapter 2: **First Vision**

Citations for this chapter are taken from Smith, *Biographical Sketches,* pp. 59–60, 61, 62–63, 64–75, 96; Quinn, *Early Mormonism,* pp. 140, 25–26, 31, 33, 42; Donna Hill, *Joseph Smith: The First Mormon* (New York, 1977), p. 45; Scot Facer Proctor and Maurine Jensen Proctor, eds., *The Revised and Enhanced History of Joseph Smith by His Mother* (Salt Lake City, 1996), p. 71 notes 2 and 3; Dean C. Jessee, ed., *The Papers of Joseph Smith: Autobiographical and Historical Writings* (Salt Lake City, 1989), I,

268; Bushman, *Joseph Smith,* pp. 32–35, 43–48, 50–51, 56, 69; Fawn M. Brodie, *No Man Knows My History: The Life of Joseph Smith* (New York, 1946), pp. 9–10, 12–13, 19–20, 25–26, Appendix A, pp. 412–417; Frances Trollope, *Domestic Manners,* I, 159, 233–246; and Joseph Smith, *History of the Church of Jesus Christ of Latter-Day Saints* (Salt Lake City, 1980), I, 4–6.

Chapter 3: Moroni

Citations for this chapter can be found in Smith, *History,* I, 20–24, 29–45, 46–47, 49–51, 52–54, 58–60, 60–64; Bushman, *Smith,* pp. 70, 76–77, 77–85; and Ephraim Hatch, "What Did Joseph Smith Look Like," quoted ibid., pp. 215–216; Smith, *Biographical Sketches,* pp. 96, 80, 87, 84, 85–86, 87–89, 104–105, 105–106; Brodie, *No Man Knows My History,* pp. 29, 30, 31–33, Appendix A, 405–407, 411; and Heidi S. Swinton, *American Prophet: The Story of Joseph Smith* (Salt Lake City, 1999), p. 55.

Chapter 4: *The Book of Mormon*

Citations for this chapter can be found in Bushman, *Smith,* pp. 86, 87–88, 104, 105–106, 108, 187–188; Joseph Smith, *History,* IV, 537–538, I, 63, 64–65, 66–72; Swinton, *American Prophet,* pp. 55–56, Hill, *Smith,* pp. 73–74, 76–77; Smith, *Biographical Sketches,* pp. 124–125, 136–139, 146–147, 148, 149; *Doctrine and Covenants* (Salt Lake City, 1981) 18; 17, hereafter cited as *D&C; Book of Mormon* (Salt Lake City, 1981), II Nephi 5:21; 6:28, 30, Mormon 9:32–33, Ether 13:6, 6:3, Moroni 10:32, 34.

Chapter 5: Organizing the Church of Christ

Citations for this chapter are taken from Remini, *Jacksonian Era,* pp. 9–20, 23–29, 70–71, 89–90; Smith, *History,* I, 51; Jessee, ed., *Papers of Smith,* I, 302–303, 304–309, 314–317, 319–323, 325, 339; Bushman, *Smith,* pp. 147–148, 168, 179, 176–177; *D&C* 21:1–6; 22:1; 25:10, 2; 24:9, 5, 3, 18; 28:2–3, 5–7, 9; 29; 3:12, 16–18; 21:1; 34:4, 17, 20, 23; 38:18–19, 12, 28, 31–33; *Book of Mormon,* Mosiah 8:17; Smith, *Bio-*

graphical Sketches, pp. 160, 161–162, 180, 187–188, 190; Hill, *Smith,* pp. 109, 46; Swinton, *American Prophet,* pp. 63–64, 74; Brodie, *No Man Knows My History,* pp. 96–97; Leonard J. Arrington and Davis Bitton, *The Mormon Experience: A History of the Latter-day Saints* (New York, 1979), pp. 28–40; Richard N. and Joan K. Ostling, *Mormon America: The Power and Promise* (San Francisco, 1999), pp. 156–157. For the "cult of domesticity" see Barbara Welter, *Dimity Convictions: The American Woman in the Nineteenth Century* (Athens, Ohio, 1976); Barbara J. Berg, *The Remembered Gate: Origins of American Feminism* (New York, 1977); and Nancy Cott, *The Bonds of Womanhood* (New York, 1977).

Chapter 6: **Kirtland**

Citations are taken from the following: Bushman, *Smith,* pp. 179, 185–187; *D&C* 50:2, 49; 45:64–66, 20; 90; 95:8–17; 102:107; 89:1, 5–21; 87:1–4; 88:119; Brodie, *No Man Knows My History,* pp. 102–103, 104–108, 181; Remini, *Jacksonian Era,* pp. 94–97, 61–68; Swinton, *American Prophet,* pp. 77, 80, 94, 92; Smith, *History,* IV, 540–541; Jessee, ed., *Papers of Smith,* I, 356–357, 360–362, 374–378; II, 209–210; Robert V. Remini, *Henry Clay: Statesman for the Union* (New York, 1991), pp. 169–192; Hill, *Smith,* pp. 142, 188, 211–212, 215; Smith, *Biographical Sketches,* pp. 213–214, 221–222; Dean C. Jessee, ed., *The Personal Writings of Joseph Smith* (Salt Lake City, 1984), pp. 351, 185; Arrington and Bitton, *Mormon Experience,* pp. 47–64. For the Bank War see Robert V. Remini, *Andrew Jackson and the Bank War* (New York, 1967).

Chapter 7: **Far West**

Citations in this chapter can be found in the following works: Remini, *Clay,* pp. 528, 562–580; Jessee, ed., *Personal Writings of Smith,* pp. 355–356; Jessee, ed., *Papers of Smith,* II, 262–263, 248, 269, 271 note 2, 287–297, and notes; *D&C* 119:1–4; Swinton, *American Prophet,* pp. 102, 106, 108–109, 116; Brodie, *No Man Knows My History,* p. 223; Hill, *Smith,* p. 229; Smith, *Biographical Sketches,* pp. 268–269, 259–265; Smith, *History,* I, 374–376; Arrington and Bitton, *Mormon Experience,* pp. 44–48.

Chapter 8: **Nauvoo**

Citations for this chapter come from Swinton, *American Prophet,* pp. 122, 140; Hill, *Smith,* pp. 271, 273, 284, 286; *D&C* 95:8–17, 124:60; 132:19, 61, 62, 52, 53; 95:8–9; Smith, *History,* VI, 303–304, 305, 308; Bushman to author, March 6, 2001; Smith, *The Pearl of Great Price* (Salt Lake City, 1981), Book of Abraham, 1–5; Eliza R. Snow, *Biography and Family Record of Lorenzo Snow* (Salt Lake City, 1884), p. 46; Remini, *Jacksonian Era,* pp. 107–110; Brodie, *No Man Knows My History,* p. 334; Ostling and Ostling, *Mormon America,* pp. 56–75, 188–190, 305; John C. Bennett, *The History of the Saints: Or an Exposé of Joseph Smith and Mormonism* (Boston, 1842; reprint, Urbana and Chicago, 1999).

Chapter 9: **Assassination**

Citations for this chapter can be found in the following works: Remini, *Jacksonian Age,* pp. 99–112; Swinton, *American Prophet,* p. 134; Hill, *Smith,* pp. 349, 292, 306, 368, 396, 399–402, 406, 411; Smith, *History,* VI, 558, 607–608; Hinckley, *What of the Mormons,* pp. 199, 202; Smith, *Biographical Sketches,* p. 298; Arrington and Bitton, *Mormon Experience,* pp. 13, 47.

SELECT BIBLIOGRAPHY

ANY BIBLIOGRAPHY of Joseph Smith must necessarily begin with his own works, the most important of which are *The Book of Mormon* (Salt Lake City, 1981); *The Doctrine and Covenants of the Church of Jesus Christ of Latter-Day Saints* (Salt Lake City, 1981); *The Pearl of Great Price* (Salt Lake City, 1981); and *History of the Church of Jesus Christ of Latter-Day Saints* (Salt Lake City, 1980), seven volumes.

Also valuable are *The Papers of Joseph Smith: Autobiographical and Historical Writings* (Salt Lake City, 1989), edited by Dean C. Jessee, two volumes; *The Personal Writings of Joseph Smith* (Salt Lake City, 1984), compiled and edited by Dean C. Jessee; and *An American Prophet's Record: The Diaries and Journals of Joseph Smith* (Salt Lake City, 1989), edited by Scott H. Faulring. See also Joseph Smith, *A Book of Commandments for the Government of the Church of Christ* (Independence, Mo., 1833); *The Holy Scriptures, Translated and Corrected by the Spirit of Revelation* (Plano, Ill., 1867); and *The Voice of Truth* (Nauvoo, Ill., 1844).

Of special value and interest are Lucy Mack Smith's *Biographical Sketches of Joseph Smith the Prophet and His Progenitors for Many Generations* (Liverpool, 1853, and Plano, Ill., 1880), and the *Revised and Enhanced History of Joseph Smith by His Mother* (Salt Lake City, 1996), edited by Scot Facer Proctor and Maurine Jensen Proctor. Brigham Young sought to suppress the 1853 edition of this book because he felt it challenged his headship of the Church.

Other documentary sources of significance include John C. Bennett, *The History of the Saints: Or an Exposé of Joe Smith and Mormonism* (Boston, 1842; reprint, Urbana and Chicago, 1999); Oliver Cowdery, *Defence in a Rehearsal of My Grounds for Separating Myself from the Latter Day Saints* (Norton, Ohio, 1839); Thomas Ford, *History of Illinois* (Chicago, 1854); Parley Parker Pratt, *Autobiography* (Chicago, 1888);

Josiah Quincy, *Figures of the Past* (Boston, 1883); Mary Ettie V. Smith, *Fifteen Years among the Mormons* (New York, 1857); and William Smith, *William Smith on Mormonism* (Lamoni, Iowa, 1883).

Secondary sources are quite voluminous and include many articles published in the *Journal of Mormon History, BYU Studies, Ensign,* and *Encyclopedia of Mormonism,* among others. Most of the biographies of Joseph Smith have been written by Mormons. Of these the best full biography is Donna Hill, *Joseph Smith: The First Mormon* (New York, 1977), although Fawn M. Brodie's critical *No Man Knows My History: The Life of Joseph Smith, the Mormon Prophet* (New York, 1946) includes a great deal of useful information and documentation not found elsewhere. Brodie was raised a Mormon, but her book brought about her excommunication from the Church. A more modern work of impressive scholarship, which unfortunately concludes with the establishment of the Church in 1830, is Richard L. Bushman's *Joseph Smith and the Beginnings of Mormonism* (Urbana and Chicago, 1984). But I found the fully documented and handsomely illustrated book by Heidi S. Swinton, *American Prophet: The Story of Joseph Smith* (Salt Lake City, 1999), based on Lee Groberg's film of the same title, to be excellent in every respect. Other biographies include Francis M. Gibbons, *Joseph Smith: Martyr, Prophet of God* (Salt Lake City, 1982); John Henry Evans, *Joseph Smith: An American Prophet* (New York, 1933); and Truman G. Madsen, *Joseph Smith the Prophet* (Salt Lake City, 1989).

For Joseph's wife, Emma Hale Smith, see Linda King Newell and Valeen Tippetts Avery, *Mormon Enigma: Emma Hale Smith* (Garden City, N.Y., 1984), and Buddy Youngreen, *Reflections of Emma, Joseph Smith's Wife* (Orem, Utah, 1982).

For particular aspects of Joseph's life see Richard Lloyd Anderson, *Joseph Smith's New England Heritage* (Salt Lake City, 1971); Milton V. Backman, *Joseph Smith's First Vision* (Salt Lake City, 1971); Larry C. Porter and Susan Easton Black, eds., *The Prophet Joseph: Essays on the Life and Mission of Joseph Smith* (Salt Lake City, 1988); D. Michael Quinn, *Early Mormonism and the Magic World View* (Salt Lake City, 1998); Grant Underwood, *The Millenarian World of Early Mormonism* (Urbana and Chicago, 1999); Larry C. Porter, *A Study of the Origins of the Church of the Latter-day Saints in the States of New York and Pennsylvania* (Salt Lake City, 2000); Milton V. Backman Jr., *The Heavens Resound: A History of the Latter-*

day Saints in Ohio, 1830–1838 (Salt Lake City, 1983); Karl Ricks Anderson, *Joseph Smith's Kirtland: Eyewitness Accounts* (Salt Lake City, 1989); Edwin B. Firmage and Richard C. Mangrum, *Zion in the Courts: A Legal History of the Church of Jesus Christ of Latter-day Saints, 1830–1900* (Urbana and Chicago, 1988); Alexander L. Baugh, *A Call to Arms: The 1838 Mormon Defense of Northern Missouri* (Salt Lake City, 2000); Leland Homer Gentry, *A History of the Latter-day Saints in Northern Missouri from 1836 to 1839* (Salt Lake City, 2000); Donald Q. Cannon and Lyndon W. Cook, *Far West Record* (Salt Lake City, 1983); Stephen C. LeSueur, *The 1838 Mormon War in Missouri* (Columbia, Mo., 1987); B. H. Roberts, *The Missouri Persecutions* (Salt Lake City, 1900); Robert Bruce Flanders, *Nauvoo: Kingdom on the Mississippi* (Urbana, Ill., 1965); Annette P. Hampshire, *Mormonism in Conflict: The Nauvoo Years* (New York, 1985); and Roger D. Launis, *Zion's Camp* (Independence, Mo., 1984).

Biographies of other leaders of the early Mormon Church include Pearson H. Corbett, *Hyrum Smith* (Salt Lake City, 1963); F. Mark McKiernan, *The Voice of One Crying in the Wilderness: Sidney Rigdon, Religious Reformer, 1793–1876* (Lawrence, Kans., 1971); Stanley R. Gunn, *Oliver Cowdery, Second Elder and Scribe* (Salt Lake City, 1962); Madge Harris Tuckett and Belle Harris Wilson, *The Martin Harris Story* (Provo, Utah, 1983); Peter L. Crowley, *The Essential Parley P. Pratt* (Salt Lake City, 1990); Stanley B. Kimball, *Heber C. Kimball: Mormon Patriarch and Pioneer* (Urbana, Ill., 1981); Leonard J. Arrington, *Brigham Young: American Moses* (New York, 1985); and Newell G. Bringhurst, *Brigham Young and the Expanding American Frontier* (Boston, 1986).

On the Second Great Awakening see Whitney R. Cross, *The Burned-Over District: The Social and Intellectual History of Enthusiastic Religions in Western New York, 1800–1850* (New York, 1950); Alice Felt Tyler, *Freedom's Ferment* (Minneapolis, 1944); Frances Trollope, *Domestic Manners of the Americans* (London, 1832); William G. McLoughlin, *Revivals, Awakenings, and Reform* (New York, 1978); and Dickson D. Bruce, *And They All Sang Hallelujah: Plain-Folk Camp-Meeting Religion, 1800–1845* (Knoxville, 1974). On Mormonism in general see Marvin S. Hill and James B. Allen, eds., *Mormonism and American Culture* (New York, 1972); Leonard J. Arrington and Davis Bitton, *The Mormon Experience: A History of the Latter-day Saints* (New York, 1979); Thomas F. O'Day, *The Mormons* (Chicago, 1957); Jan Shipps, *Mormonism: The Story of a New*

Religious Tradition (Urbana and Chicago, 1985); and Richard N. and Joan K. Ostling, *Mormon America: The Power and the Promise* (San Francisco, 1999).

For a general account of the Jacksonian age I have used my own study *The Jacksonian Era* (Arlington Heights, Ill., 1989) along with Harry L. Watson, *Liberty and Power: The Politics of Jacksonian America* (New York, 1990); Daniel Feller, *The Jacksonian Promise: America, 1815–1840* (Baltimore, 1995); Jack Larkin, *The Reshaping of Everyday Life, 1790–1840* (New York, 1988); Barbara Welter, *Dimity Convictions: The American Woman in the Nineteenth Century* (Athens, Ohio, 1976); Barbara J. Berg, *The Remembered Gate: Origins of American Feminism* (New York, 1977); Nancy Cott, *The Bonds of Womanhood* (New York, 1977); Robert V. Remini, *Andrew Jackson and the Bank War* (New York, 1967); and Robert V. Remini, *Henry Clay: Statesman for the Union* (New York, 1991).